Savories and Sweets

from

THE UNCOMMON GOURMET

For Charlie—
Cook, create, and celebrate!..
Ellen

ELLEN HELMAN

Published by
Font & Center Press
69 Pinecroft Road
Weston, MA 02193
www.fontandcenter.com

ISBN: 978-1-883280-21-5

First Printing 2013
Published in the United States of America
1 2 3 4 5 6 7 8 9 10

ACKNOWLEDGEMENTS

I want to extend my most heartfelt thanks to all who have encouraged, inspired, and supported me throughout this project. Without you all I would not have been able to realize my dream.

To my loving husband, Robert

To my wonderful children:
Jen and Sam
Lee and Amy

To my darling grandchildren:
Max, Peggy, and Benjamin

To my littlest loves:
Spencer and Sadie
M and P

To my devoted in-laws, Bucky and Bubsy

To my loyal fans and taste testers who willing tried new creations

And a special dedication to Viv and Jookie
for always being in my heart and in my thoughts

I love you all!

OTHER BOOKS BY ELLEN HELMAN

The Uncommon Gourmet

The Uncommon Gourmet's All-Occasion Cookbook

Home Cooking with The Uncommon Gourmet

TABLE OF

CONTENTS

INTRODUCTION

Welcome to *Savories and Sweets*!

The inspiration for this book was born out of my desire to excite people's tastes and cater to their food preferences. Having been involved in the food field for more than twenty-five years—as a food writer, cookbook author, caterer, and teacher—I have observed that when given a choice, people prefer eating any array of small bites as opposed to an entire meal. With that in mind, I have created a collection of recipes that encompasses savory appetizers, artful salads, and indulgent desserts.

Following in the footsteps of its predecessors, the recipes in this book are structured to be simple, straightforward, and streamlined. Use only the best, freshest quality ingredients available, as a recipe is only as good as its components.

Savories and Sweets was conceived with my love and passion for creating, cooking, and sharing. The cooking experience nourishes the soul, so read, experiment, and most of all, enjoy this newest edition from the "Uncommon Gourmet."

To tastes, truffles, and triumphs!

Wishing you all kitchen success.

Ellen Helman

TABLE OF RECIPES

PRELUDES

DIPS AND SPREADS

SIPPERS

WAFERS AND BRUSCHETTA

TARTLETS AND FILLED PASTRIES

SMALL BITES

MEAT AND CHICKEN TIDBITS

SEAFOOD MORSELS

INTERLUDES

GARDEN GREENERY

PASTA, BEAN, AND GRAIN SALADS

HEARTY SALADS

FINALES

FRUITS, PUDDINGS, AND CRISPS

COOKIES, BARS, AND BISCOTTI

CAKES, PIES, AND PASTRIES

CHOCOLATE INDULGENCES

HELPFUL HINTS

A recipe is only as good as its ingredients. I can not stress emphatically enough how important it is to use the freshest, best quality products available. The better the quality of the ingredients, the better the end results!

The following guidelines will help make cooking from ***Savories and Sweets*** a successful experience.

1. Always read through a recipe before beginning to make sure you have all the ingredients and understand the procedure.

2. Always preheat your oven, especially before baking.

3. It is important to use the correct pan size, especially when baking, to achieve good results.

4. All herbs called for are fresh unless otherwise noted.

5. Lemon juice is always fresh, never bottled.

6. When using vanilla, make sure it's pure vanilla extract, not imitation.

7. Use unsalted butter in all recipes calling for butter. That way you can control the amount of salt in the recipe.

8. Use extra-large eggs in all cooking and baking. Egg size does matter, especially when baking.

9. I no longer use vegetable oil when cooking or baking. Instead I use different grades of olive oil; I prefer its flavor and it's a healthier choice. I use light or plain olive oil when baking, sautéing, and in some salad dressings; I use extra-virgin olive oil in marinades, sauces, and salad dressings.

10. Make all salad dressings at least 30 minutes in advance (and preferably up to 24 hours) to allow the flavors to blend.

11. When making salad dressings, if you prefer a stronger garlic flavor than what I've suggested, mince the garlic into the dressing instead of smashing the clove and removing it before serving.

PRELUDES

Appetizers and hors d'oeuvres are the meal openers, meant to amuse and delight you. They excite the palate, awaken the taste buds, and stimulate the appetite. They span a wide spectrum—from trendy hand-held nibbles to dips and hearty kebobs. Hors d'oeuvres are the popular, go-to foods at parties and gatherings. They're the whimsical part of the meal that is consumed with pleasure. The more unusual and tantalizing the appetizer, the greater its appeal. People will sooner gravitate to interesting tartlets and bruschetta than to a wedge of cheese.

Remember, we taste with our eyes before we sample with our palate. Therefore, it is important to make the food colorful, fanciful, and enticing, like an artist's palette. Flavors should be lush and aromas mouth-watering, sparking one's interest.

A good rule of thumb when entertaining is to allow 2 to 3 pieces of each type of hors d'oeuvre per person. Variety is the spice of life, so offer your guests an array of foods, balancing the choices. Make some vegetable, some meat, chicken, or seafood, others bruschetta, or cheese.

Celebrate the occasion with an exciting and savory display of small bites and let the partying begin.

DIPS AND SPREADS

AVOCADO DIP

NOTATIONS

This creamy, mouth-watering avocado spread is reminiscent of guacamole with the added enhancement of garlic, cumin, and cilantro.

2 ripe Haas avocados, pitted and peeled
1/2 cup sour cream
2 tablespoons diced red onion
1 large clove garlic, minced
2 tablespoons chopped cilantro
1/2 teaspoon ground cumin
1/8 teaspoon cayenne pepper
2 tablespoons lemon juice
salt to taste

1. In a bowl, mash the avocados with a fork, leaving them somewhat chunky.

2. Add the remaining ingredients and mix until evenly blended. Serve with tortilla chips, pita chips, or vegetables.

2 cups

CHILI DIP

The fiery flavors indigenous to chili are wrapped up in this creamy kidney bean dip. Chili powder, the traditional backbone of many Mexican dishes, is what gives the dip its rich flavor and color. It's especially good served with tortilla chips.

NOTATIONS

14- to 15-ounce can red kidney beans, rinsed and drained
1/2 cup sour cream
1 large clove garlic, crushed
salt and freshly ground pepper to taste
1 1/2 tablespoons chili powder
1 1/2 teaspoons ground cumin
1 teaspoon ground coriander
1/4 to 1/2 teaspoon cayenne pepper
2 tablespoons lime juice

1. Put all of the ingredients in the bowl of a food processor and purée.

2. Remove the dip to a bowl, surround with tortilla chips, and serve.

about 1 1/2 cups

GREEN OLIVE HUMMUS

NOTATIONS

I've stepped up the traditional hummus that Americans have come to love. Manzanilla olives, the pimiento-stuffed green olives, lend piquancy to the Middle Eastern chickpea dip, giving it a new twist and making it even more dazzling.

15 to 16-ounce can chickpeas, rinsed and drained
2/3 cup small Manzanilla olives
1 large clove garlic, crushed
salt and freshly ground pepper to taste
2 tablespoons lemon juice
1/3 cup extra-virgin olive oil

1. Put all of the ingredients in the bowl of a food processor and purée.

2. Transfer the hummus to a bowl, surround with pita bread and vegetables, and serve. (This may be prepared up to 24 hours in advance and refrigerated. Return to room temperature to serve.)

1 2/3 cups

PUMPKIN HUMMUS

This is the ultimate, over the top, savory hummus. Puréed chickpeas and pumpkin are perfumed with cumin, cinnamon, and coriander and redolent with garlic. Its fragrance is intoxicating and it's so delicious.

NOTATIONS

15 to 16-ounce can chickpeas, rinsed and drained
1 cup canned pumpkin purée
salt and freshly ground pepper to taste
1 large clove garlic, crushed
3/4 teaspoon ground cumin
1/2 teaspoon cinnamon
1/2 teaspoon ground coriander
3 tablespoons lemon juice
6 tablespoons extra-virgin olive oil

1. Put all of the ingredients in the bowl of a food processor and purée.

2. Remove to a bowl and surround with pita bread or pita chips, cucumber rounds, and carrots.

2½ cups

MUHAMMARA

NOTATIONS

Muhammara is a typical Turkish spread resplendent with roasted peppers and walnuts and perfumed with pomegranate syrup. It's savory and dazzling with flavor! I accompany this with wedges of pita bread or pita chips.

2 large roasted red peppers, coarsely chopped
2/3 cup chopped walnuts, toasted
2/3 cup French bread crumbs, toasted
1 large clove garlic, crushed
salt to taste
1 teaspoon ground cumin
1/2 teaspoon crushed red pepper flakes
2 teaspoons Grenadine
2 tablespoons lemon juice
1/4 cup extra-virgin olive oil

1. Put all of the ingredients in the bowl of a food processor and purée.

2. Remove to a bowl and let sit at room temperature for 2 to 3 hours for the flavors to blend, and as much as overnight in the refrigerator. (Return to room temperature to serve.)

about 1 3/4 cups

WHITE BEAN DIP

NOTATIONS

This simple to prepare cannellini bean purée is distinguished by a swirl of lusty pesto. I like to serve it with slices of French bread and an array of crudités.

1½ cups canned cannellini beans, rinsed and drained
½ cup pesto (recipe follows)
salt to taste
2 tablespoons lemon juice
2 tablespoons extra-virgin olive oil

1. Put all of the ingredients in the bowl of a food processor and purée.

2. Transfer the dip to a bowl, surround with fresh vegetables and bread or crackers and serve.

about 1¾ cups

Pesto:
1 cup firmly packed fresh basil
½ cup pine nuts, toasted
1 to 2 cloves garlic, crushed
salt to taste
6 tablespoons grated Parmigiano-Reggiano cheese
½ cup extra-virgin olive oil

1. Put the basil, pine nuts, garlic, salt, and cheese in the bowl of a food processor and grind to a paste.

2. With the motor running, add the oil in a slow, steady stream until completely incorporated. Transfer the pesto to a container and store in the refrigerator for up to 1 week.

1 cup of pesto

NOTATIONS

CRANBERRY-CHÈVRE SPREAD

This goat cheese-based spread is resplendent with dried cranberries, orange zest, and cinnamon and is spiked with Amaretto. I like to serve it with slices of pears and bruschetta. It also doubles as an outstanding stuffing for chicken breasts.

8 ounces chèvre, crumbled
1/2 cup dried cranberries
2 teaspoons finely grated orange zest
1/4 teaspoon cinnamon
2 tablespoons Amaretto
1 tablespoon finely chopped almonds, toasted

1. In a bowl, combine the chèvre, cranberries, orange zest, cinnamon, and Amaretto and mix well. Refrigerate for 3 to 4 hours and as much as 24 hours for flavors to blend.

2. When ready to serve, return to room temperature. Sprinkle the top with toasted almonds and present.

6 to 8 portions

CURRIED CREAM CHEESE SPREAD

NOTATIONS

This heavenly Indian-inspired spread is the stuff of which dreams are made. Cream cheese is infused with raisins, coconut, curry, and ginger and is guaranteed to romance your senses. It also makes a luscious stuffing for chicken breasts.

8 ounces cream cheese, at room temperature
1 teaspoon curry powder
3 tablespoons sweetened, shredded coconut, toasted
3 tablespoons raisins
1½ tablespoons minced, candied, crystallized ginger
1 French bread, cut into ½-inch thick rounds, toasted

1. In a bowl with an electric mixer, blend the cream cheese and curry.

2. Add the coconut, raisins, and ginger and mix until evenly blended. (This may be made up to 24 hours in advance and refrigerated. Return to room temperature to serve.)

3. Surround the spread with the French bread rounds and present.

about 1½ cups

HERRING PÂTÉ

NOTATIONS

Russian flavors predominate in this creamy spread that elevates pickled herring to new heights. I like to serve it with pumpernickel bread.

6-ounce jar pickled herring, drained
6 ounces cream cheese, at room temperature
2 tablespoons minced red onion
1 teaspoon white horseradish
freshly ground pepper to taste
1 tablespoon chopped dill
1 tablespoon finely chopped parsley

1. Measure 1 cup of herring pieces and place them in the bowl of a food processor. (Save the rest for another time.)

2. Add the remaining ingredients to the food processor and purée until creamy. (This may be made up to 24 hours in advance and refrigerated. Return to room temperature to serve.) Remove to a bowl, surround with bread, and serve.

about 1¼ cups

SIPPERS

NOTATIONS

POMOSA

This drink is modeled after the infamous Mimosa which consists of equal parts orange juice and Champagne. This fashionable mix combines pomegranate juice and Prosecco, an Italian sparkling wine. The result is a ruby-hued, effervescent, and deliciously fruity cocktail that's perfect for brunches, luncheons, and parties.

1 (750 ml) bottle Prosecco, chilled
3¼ cups POM (pomegranate juice), chilled
2 tablespoons Grenadine

1. In a large pitcher, combine all of the ingredients and stir well.
2. Pour into champagne flutes and serve.

8 portions

RASPBERRY BELLINI

Harry's Bar in Venice, Italy is credited with putting the Bellini on the map. Classically, a Bellini is a delightful peach nectar and sparkling wine drink. I have put a new spin on the traditional, infusing the peach cocktail with raspberry essence.

1 (750 ml) bottle Prosecco, chilled
1/4 cup peach schnapps
1 1/2 cups (6 ounces) raspberries, puréed
2 tablespoons raspberry jam, melted

1. Pour the Prosecco and peach schnapps into a large pitcher.

2. In a small bowl, combine the puréed raspberries and jam, mixing until evenly blended.

3. Add the purée to the pitcher, stir well, pour into champagne flutes, and serve.

5 to 6 portions

NOTATIONS

SANGRÍA

NOTATIONS

Sangría is the fruity wine drink that originated in Spain. This white wine-based version is light, ambrosial, and refreshing. Always serve it well-chilled.

3 ripe peaches, peeled, pitted, and each cut into 8 wedges
1/2 navel orange, sliced
3 tablespoons superfine sugar
1 (750 ml) bottle Pinot Grigio wine, chilled
2 tablespoons Triple Sec
2 cups Perrier or other sparkling water, chilled

1. Put half of the peach wedges in the bowl of a food processor and purée.

2. Put the remaining peach wedges and orange slices in a large pitcher. Sprinkle with sugar, mix well, and let sit for 10 minutes for the sugar to dissolve.

3. Add the puréed peaches, wine, and Triple Sec and stir well. Refrigerate until ready to serve.

4. Add the sparkling water, mix well, and serve in tall glasses.

6 portions

DARK AND STORMY

A Dark and Stormy is one of my husband's favorite mixed drinks. He particularly enjoys sipping them on a hot summer's night. The highball's basic components are dark rum, specifically Gosling's black rum, and ginger beer. Served over ice with a twist of lime, it's spicy, cooling, and refreshing.

NOTATIONS

ice
1/4 cup (2 ounces) dark rum
1 cup (8 ounces) ginger beer
twist of lime

1. Fill a highball glass with ice.
2. Pour the rum over the ice. Add the ginger beer and stir well.
3. Garnish with a twist of lime and enjoy.

1 drink

MANGO GAZPACHO

NOTATIONS

Modeled after the popular Spanish soup, this fruity rendition offers Mexican flavors that are both lively and satisfying.

2 ripe mangoes, peeled, pitted, and chopped
1 large yellow pepper, chopped
1 medium-size cucumber, peeled and chopped
½ cup diced Vidalia or other sweet onion
1 large clove garlic, crushed
3 tablespoons finely chopped cilantro
salt and freshly ground pepper to taste
2 tablespoons lime juice
2 tablespoons extra-virgin olive oil
2 cups mango juice or mango juice blend

1. Put the mangoes, pepper, cucumber, onion, garlic, cilantro, salt, pepper, lime juice, oil, and 1 cup of mango juice in a blender or the bowl of a food processor and pulse to a chunky purée.

2. Remove the mixture to a large bowl. Add the remaining 1 cup of mango juice, stir well, and refrigerate for 1 to 2 hours to allow flavors to blend. (This may be made up to 24 hours in advance.)

3. Bring the soup to room temperature and serve.

4 portions

STRAWBERRY SOUP

Cool and refreshing, this pink-hued soup is perfect for the dog days of summer. It also makes a sublime sipper, served up in cordial glasses.

1 quart ripe strawberries, hulled and coarsely chopped
2 tablespoons strawberry preserves
1 cup sour cream
1 cup cranberry juice

1. Put all of the ingredients in a blender and purée.
2. Chill until serving time. Ladle into bowls and serve.

4 portions

NOTATIONS

CREAM OF TOMATO SOUP

NOTATIONS

A bowl of creamy tomato soup is old-fashioned comfort food. Served hot, this soup is most satisfying and delicious. (It's also refreshing served chilled on a hot summer day.)

8-ounce can stewed tomatoes
2 cups V-8 juice
2 tablespoons lemon juice
salt and freshly ground pepper to taste
1/4 teaspoon Worcestershire sauce
pinch of cayenne pepper or more to taste
2 tablespoons chopped scallions
1/2 cup sour cream
extra sour cream for garnish

1. Put all of the ingredients (except the sour cream for garnish) in a blender and purée.

2. Transfer the soup to a saucepan and heat gently—do not let the soup boil, as the sour cream will curdle. When hot, ladle into bowls, garnish each portion with a dollop of sour cream, and serve.

4 portions

PUMPKIN SOUP

NOTATIONS

This creamy, orange-hued autumnal soup is warm and comforting. Scented with ginger and garnished with crème fraîche, it makes a wonderful beginning to the Thanksgiving feast.

2 tablespoons unsalted butter
1 medium-size yellow onion, chopped
1 large clove garlic, crushed
16-ounce can pumpkin purée
3 cups chicken broth
salt and freshly ground pepper to taste
1/2 teaspoon ground ginger
1 1/2 teaspoons dark brown sugar
1/2 cup light cream
crème fraîche for garnish

1. Heat the butter in a large saucepan. Add the onion and sauté over medium heat until soft and translucent. Add the garlic and sauté for 1 minute more.

2. Add the pumpkin, broth, salt, pepper, ginger, and brown sugar. Bring to a boil, lower the heat, and simmer uncovered for 10 minutes.

3. Stir in the cream and heat gently. Serve at once, garnishing each portion with a dollop of crème fraîche.

4 to 6 portions

WAFERS AND BRUSCHETTA

LEMON-THYME BISCOTTI

NOTATIONS

Unlike the sweet, crunchy cookie we know as biscotti, these savory pastries are more like biscuits. Redolent with lemon, thyme, and chives, these crispy crackers are great for casual munching with glasses of wine.

1/2 cup unsalted butter, at room temperature
2 ounces chèvre, at room temperature
3 tablespoons sugar
2 eggs
1 tablespoon finely grated lemon zest
2 tablespoons chopped chives
1 1/4 teaspoons dried thyme
2 cups all-purpose flour
1 1/2 teaspoons baking powder
1/2 teaspoon salt

1. Preheat the oven to 350°. Line a baking sheet with parchment paper.

2. In a large bowl with an electric mixer, cream the butter, chèvre, and sugar.

3. Add the eggs, lemon zest, chives, and thyme and beat until fluffy.

4. Add the flour, baking powder, and salt and beat only until the mixture comes together. Turn the dough out onto the parchment-lined baking sheet and form into a log, 10 inches long.

5. Bake for 30 minutes. Remove the log with the parchment paper to a wooden board to cool for 10 minutes. Cut on the diagonal into 5/8-inch wide slices. (Trim off the tiny end slices.) Place a rack on the baking sheet and place the slices on the rack, 1/2-inch apart.

6. Return the biscotti to the oven and bake for 20 minutes. Remove the biscuits to a rack to cool completely.

about 14 biscotti

HERBED FETA CROSTINI

Tangy feta cheese joins forces with zatar, creating a most dazzling spread atop French bread rounds. Zatar is a seasoning blend of sumac, thyme, and sesame seeds, indigenous to Middle Eastern cuisine.

6 ounces feta cheese, crumbled
3/4 teaspoon zatar
freshly ground pepper to taste
2 tablespoons extra-virgin olive oil
10 slices French bread, cut 3/4-inch thick

1. Preheat the oven to 400°.

2. In a bowl, combine the feta, zatar, pepper, and olive oil and mix until evenly blended.

3. Spread 1 1/2 tablespoons of the cheese mixture atop each bread round. Place on a baking sheet.

4. Bake for 10 minutes until golden. Serve hot from the oven.

10 crostini

NOTATIONS

LEMON FRICOS

NOTATIONS

Crisp and fragrant with lemon, these zesty Parmesan wafers are wonderful cocktail nibbles. They also make a tasty garnish for salads.

1½ cups packed, grated Parmigiano-Reggiano cheese
1 tablespoon finely grated lemon zest
½ teaspoon crushed red pepper flakes

1. Preheat the oven to 350°. Line two baking sheets with parchment paper.

2. In a bowl, combine all of the ingredients and mix well.

3. Using 2 tablespoons of the mixture, form into a 2-inch round on the prepared pan. Space the mounds 3 inches apart.

4. Bake for about 10 minutes until golden. Let the fricos sit on the baking sheet for 2 minutes before removing them to a rack to cool completely.

12 fricos; 4 to 6 portions

APPLE-CHEDDAR PUFFS

NOTATIONS

Apples and cheddar are a dynamic classic pairing. We usually think of sliced apple paired with wedges of cheese. This combination takes it one step further, featuring grated fruit and cheese punctuated with red onion. Piled high atop French bread rounds and baked until puffed and golden, these bruschetta are a real crowd pleaser.

3/4 cup coarsely grated sharp cheddar cheese
2/3 cup peeled and coarsely grated Granny Smith apple
1/3 cup diced red onion
pinch of nutmeg
1/2 cup mayonnaise
12 slices (3/4-inch thick) French bread rounds

1. Preheat the oven to 400°.

2. In a bowl, combine the cheese, apple, onion, nutmeg, and mayonnaise and mix until evenly combined.

3. Spread 2 tablespoons of the mixture atop each bread round. Place on a baking sheet.

4. Bake for 12 to 15 minutes until puffed and golden. Serve at once.

6 portions

BLUE CHEESE-OLIVE PUFFS

NOTATIONS

The combination of blue cheese and pimiento-stuffed green olives in these puffs is a gastronomic thrill—sharp, tangy, salty, and very satisfying.

3/4 cup chopped pimiento-stuffed green olives
2/3 cup crumbled blue cheese
1/2 cup diced red onion
1/2 cup mayonnaise
4 English muffins, split in half

1. Preheat the oven to 400°.

2. In a bowl, combine the olives, blue cheese, onion, and mayonnaise and mix until evenly blended.

3. Spread equal amounts of the mixture atop each muffin half. Cut each muffin round into quarters. (This may be prepared up to 24 hours in advance and refrigerated. Return to room temperature before baking.) Place on a baking sheet.

4. Bake for 15 minutes until browned and puffed. Serve at once.

6 to 8 portions

HERBED MINI SCONES

NOTATIONS

Biscuit-like, herb-scented, and filled with goat cheese, these flaky mini scones are sure to capture your attention.

2 cups all-purpose flour
1 tablespoon baking powder
$1/2$ teaspoon salt
2 tablespoons sugar
1 teaspoon herbs de Provence
$1\frac{1}{3}$ cups heavy cream
Chèvre Filling (recipe follows)

1. Preheat the oven to 425°.

2. In a large bowl, combine the flour, baking powder, salt, sugar, and herbs and mix well.

3. Add the cream and stir until the dough comes together. With lightly floured hands, turn the dough out onto a floured board. Knead gently just until the dough comes together. Pat into an 8-inch square. Cut into 25 pieces.

4. Place the squares on an ungreased baking sheet, 2 inches apart.

5. Bake in the upper third of the oven for 12 to 14 minutes until puffed and golden. Remove to a rack to cool slightly. While still warm (or if you prefer at room temperature) split the scones in half. Spread the bottom halves with the chèvre filling, cover with the tops of the scones, and serve.

25 mini scones

Chèvre Filling:
6 ounces chèvre, at room temperature
2 tablespoons heavy cream
2 tablespoons chopped chives

In a small bowl, mix the chèvre, cream, and chives until evenly blended. (This may be prepared 24 hours in advance and refrigerated. Return to room temperature before using.)

Note—this spread is also delicious slathered on bruschetta and topped with smoked salmon, tomatoes, prosciutto, or thinly sliced cucumber.

NOTATIONS

BRUSCHETTA WITH RICOTTA AND FIG JAM

I am particularly fond of pairing dried fruits and nuts; they have a natural affinity. These bruschetta are resplendent with a savory fig jam that's garnished with chopped hazelnuts. Any extra fig spread will keep for 2 to 3 weeks in the refrigerator. It's wonderful with roasted or grilled chicken and pork, and doubles as a sandwich spread with roasted turkey, ham, and prosciutto with cheese.

12 (3/4-inch thick) slices French bread
1/2 cup ricotta cheese
6 tablespoons Fig Jam (recipe follows)
6 tablespoons chopped hazelnuts

1. Preheat the oven to 400°.

2. Spread the ricotta evenly among the bread rounds. Top each with 1/2 tablespoon of fig jam. Sprinkle with the chopped nuts.

3. Bake in the oven for 8 to 10 minutes until warm. Serve hot or warm.

4 to 6 portions

Fig Jam:
1 cup coarsely chopped dried Calimyrna figs
1/2 cup balsamic vinegar
1/3 cup water
2 tablespoons sugar
2 tablespoons diced red onion

1. Put all of the ingredients in a saucepan and bring to a boil. Reduce the heat and simmer for 15 minutes. Let cool completely.

2. Put the mixture in the bowl of a food processor and purée. Store in the refrigerator until needed.

about 1 cup

TOMATO BRUSCHETTA

NOTATIONS

This version of the infamous Italian finger food gives new definition to an old standard. Rounds of French bread are daubed with pesto, topped with slow-roasted tomatoes, sprinkled with chèvre, and finished with a balsamic glaze. Slow-roasting the tomatoes concentrates and intensifies their rich flavor. This definitely has the yummy factor.

6 medium-size plum tomatoes, cut in half through the core
1 to 1½ tablespoons extra-virgin olive oil
sea salt to taste
½ teaspoon dried basil
12 (¾-inch thick) slices French bread
6 tablespoons pesto (See recipe page 10)
3 ounces chèvre, crumbled
⅓ cup balsamic vinegar, reduced to 2 tablespoons (recipe follows)

1. Preheat the oven to 300°. Line a baking sheet with parchment paper.

2. Place the tomatoes cut side up on the prepared baking sheet. Drizzle with olive oil, season with salt, and sprinkle with basil.

3. Roast for 2 hours. Remove from the oven and set aside. (This may be prepared up to 8 hours in advance.)

4. When ready to serve, preheat the oven to 400°.

5. Spread about ½ tablespoon of pesto on top of each bread round. Top with a tomato half, cut side up. Sprinkle each with crumbled chèvre. Place on a baking sheet.

6. Bake for 12 minutes until the cheese melts. Remove to a platter, drizzle the tops with the balsamic reduction, and serve.

4 to 6 portions

Balsamic Reduction:
⅓ cup balsamic vinegar

Put the balsamic vinegar in a small saucepan. Bring to a boil, reduce the heat, and let simmer slowly for 6 to 7 minutes until syrupy and reduced to 2 tablespoons. Remove from the heat and let cool. (This may be made up to 1 week in advance and stored in an air-tight container.)

TARTLETS AND FILLED PASTRIES

BREAD CUPS

NOTATIONS

These bread cups are even better than sliced bread! Cookie cutter rounds of white sandwich bread are molded into mini-tart pans and then baked until golden, creating the perfect vessel for filling with a host of ingredients. I like to keep a batch in the freezer for spontaneous entertaining.

18 slices white sandwich bread (I use Pepperidge Farm.)
PAM or other cooking oil spray

1. Preheat the oven to 400°. Grease a mini-tart pan.

2. Using a 2½-inch round cookie cutter, cut a round from the middle of each slice of bread. (Save the scraps to make bread crumbs.)

3. Place the rounds on a cutting board. Flatten the rounds with a rolling pin.

4. Place each round into a well of the prepared tart pan. Press the bread into place with your fingers to conform to the shape of the cup.

5. Spray the bread with PAM.

6. Bake for 6 to 7 minutes until the edges are golden. Remove the bread tartlets from the pan to a rack to cool completely before filling.

18 bread cups

FILLING IDEAS FOR BREAD CUPS

NOTATIONS

For a tantalizing finger food, be creative and fill bread cups with any one of the following combinations. Watch how fast they disappear!

- Blue cheese, cream cheese, and bacon
- Ratatouille
- Mascarpone cheese, diced figs, and chopped prosciutto
- Chopped tomatoes, diced buffalo mozzarella, and pesto
- Chicken salad
- Egg salad with caviar
- Guacamole
- Hummus or pumpkin hummus
- Chèvre, horseradish, and diced beets
- Smoked salmon, cream cheese, chives, and dill
- Pâté
- Tuna tartare
- Goat cheese, pesto, and chopped sun-dried tomatoes
- Muhammara
- Cooked sausage meat and diced roasted peppers
- Cream cheese, dried cranberries, toasted walnuts, and orange zest
- Chopped bacon, chopped tomato, and cheddar cheese
- Peanut butter and jelly
- Corn niblets, black beans, and salsa
- Manchego cheese and guava jelly
- Baba ghanoush
- Tapenade
- Chopped shrimp and chopped artichoke hearts with mustard mayonnaise
- White bean dip
- Chopped shrimp with Russian dressing
- Feta, olives, and roasted peppers
- Mascarpone, chopped dates, toasted pecans, and chopped candied ginger

BLUE CHEESE-FIG TARTLETS

NOTATIONS

Blue cheese and figs are a magical combination—the pungent, sharp cheese enhances the sweet, dried fruit. Punctuated with toasted walnuts and red onion, the contrasting flavors in these tartlets are divine.

2 ounces blue cheese, crumbled
3 tablespoons finely diced dried figs
2 tablespoons finely chopped walnuts, toasted
1 tablespoon finely minced red onion
1 tablespoon agave nectar
16 bread cups (See recipe page 37)

1. Preheat the oven to 350°.

2. In a bowl, combine the cheese, figs, walnuts, onion, and agave nectar and mix well until evenly blended.

3. Fill each bread cup with 1/2 tablespoon of the mixture. Put the bread cups on a baking sheet.

4. Heat in the oven for 5 to 6 minutes until warm. Serve at once.

6 to 8 portions

BRIE TARTLETS

Brie is the rich, buttery, soft-ripening French cheese Americans have come to love. Presented in bread cups with luxurious toppings, it's the ultimate small bite.

NOTATIONS

2 tablespoons dried cranberries
3 tablespoons apricot preserves
2 tablespoons chopped almonds
1/8 pound Brie cheese (weight after white rind is removed), cut into 10 pieces
10 bread cups (See recipe page 37)

1. Preheat the oven to 350°.

2. In a bowl, combine the cranberries, preserves, and almonds and mix well.

3. Fill each bread cup with a piece of Brie. Top the cheese with a spoonful of the preserve mixture. Place the tartlets on a baking sheet.

4. Bake in the oven for 10 to 12 minutes until cheese is warm and melted. Serve at once.

4 to 6 portions

NOTATIONS

BRIE TARTLET TOPPINGS

Brie-filled bread cups provide the perfect base for a myriad of toppings. Try adding these embellishments to the cheese base before baking for a sparkling hors d'oeuvre.

- Diced figs and honey
- Diced pears drizzled with a balsamic glaze
- Chopped dried apricots and chopped pistachio nuts
- Whole berry cranberry sauce and orange zest
- Ratatouille
- Mango chutney
- Olivada
- Chopped walnuts and maple syrup
- Pesto and pine nuts
- Chopped sun-dried tomatoes and chopped prosciutto
- Ginger preserves
- Red onion jam
- Orange marmalade and almonds
- Cooked sausage meat and honey mustard

CHÈVRE TARTLETS

NOTATIONS

The aromatic blend of herbs de Provence perfumes these warm, chèvre-filled bread cups. Garnished with a dusting of pistachios, they're dreamy.

4 ounces chèvre, crumbled
1 tablespoon honey
1 teaspoon herbs de Provence
16 bread cups (See recipe page 37)
4 teaspoons finely chopped pistachio nuts

1. Preheat the oven to 400°.

2. In a bowl, combine the chèvre, honey, and herbs and mix until evenly blended.

3. Fill each bread cup with 1/2 tablespoon of the mixture. Sprinkle each with 1/4 teaspoon of pistachios. Put the tartlets on a baking sheet.

4. Heat in the oven for 6 to 7 minutes until warm. Serve at once.

6 to 8 portions

CRAB TARTLETS

NOTATIONS

The flavors of deviled crab cakes are nestled in mini-tart shells for pop-in-the-mouth pleasure.

1/2 pound lump crabmeat
2 tablespoons diced scallion
3 tablespoons diced roasted red pepper
3 tablespoons mayonnaise
2 teaspoons Dijon mustard
1/2 teaspoon Worcestershire sauce
1/2 teaspoon Old Bay Seasoning
pinch of cayenne pepper
20 bread cups (See recipe page 37)

1. In a bowl, combine the crabmeat, scallion, roasted pepper, mayonnaise, Dijon, Worcestershire sauce, and seasonings and mix well until evenly blended. (This may be prepared up to 8 hours in advance and refrigerated. Return to room temperature to serve.)

2. Fill each bread cup with 1 tablespoon of the mixture. Serve at room temperature.

6 to 8 portions

SPANOKOPITA TARTLETS

Spanokopita is the traditional Greek hors d'oeuvre of phyllo-wrapped spinach and cheese pastries. Bread cups sport the same, infamous filling, making this appetizer an easy, go-to choice.

NOTATIONS

9-ounce package frozen, chopped spinach, thawed and squeezed of its excess liquid
½ cup crumbled feta cheese
2 tablespoons chopped scallion
½ teaspoon dried dill
15 bread cups (See recipe page 37)

1. Preheat the oven to 350°.

2. In a bowl, combine the spinach, feta, scallion, and dill and stir until evenly mixed.

3. Fill each bread cup with a spoonful of the mixture, pressing down gently.

4. Put the filled cups on a baking sheet.

5. Bake for 10 minutes. Serve at once.

6 to 8 portions

WONTON CUPS

NOTATIONS

Cookie cutter rounds of wonton wraps are molded into mini muffin pans, baked until golden, then filled with a host of imaginative combinations. These cups make the perfect finger food for cocktail parties.

48 wonton wraps
PAM or other cooking oil spray

1. Preheat the oven to 400°. Grease mini muffin pans.

2. Place 2 wonton skins together. Using a 2½-inch round cookie cutter, cut a round through both layers of wontons. Discard the edges.

3. Place the double-thick round into a well of the muffin pan. Gently press the round to conform to the shape of the pan. Spray the wrap with PAM. Repeat with the remaining wraps.

4. Bake for 6 to 7 minutes until golden. Remove the cups from the pan to a rack to cool completely before filling. (I like to make a batch of these and keep them in the freezer for unexpected company.)

2 dozen wonton cups

FILLING IDEAS FOR WONTON CUPS

NOTATIONS

Wonton cups make the ultimate finger food for parties and gatherings. They provide the perfect backdrop for a variety of fillings. The combinations are only as limited as your imagination! Be adventurous and try some of the following ideas.

- Egg salad
- Green olive hummus
- Pâté
- Salsa
- Diced dried figs, mascarpone cheese, and orange marmalade
- Smoked salmon, sour cream, and caviar
- Diced cucumber, feta, and mint
- Caponata
- Prosciutto, chopped tomato, and diced buffalo mozzarella
- Cream cheese, chopped dates, and chopped walnuts
- Jack cheese, cream cheese, and hot pepper jelly
- Chopped dates, chopped bacon, and diced candied, crystallized ginger
- Chopped shrimp with tarragon mayonnaise

Another option is to fill the cups, then warm them in a 350° oven for 5 minutes before presenting. The following combinations are delicious served warm.

- Cream cheese and olivada
- Chopped salami, grated cheddar cheese, and Dijon mustard
- Brie, cranberry sauce, and chopped almonds
- Bacon, blue cheese, and chopped pecans
- Cooked sausage, roasted peppers, and grated mozzarella cheese
- Diced apple, grated cheddar cheese, and chopped walnuts

WONTONS BALAZAR

NOTATIONS

These wonton skins are replete with a sumptuous horseradish-chèvre filling. The characteristic heady flavor of the cheese pairs well with the sharpness of the horseradish.

4 ounces chèvre, crumbled
1½ tablespoons prepared white horseradish
freshly ground pepper to taste
16 wonton wraps
1 tablespoon olive oil (not extra-virgin)

1. Preheat the oven to 400°. Grease two baking pans.

2. In a bowl, combine the chèvre, horseradish, and pepper and mix well.

3. Place ½ tablespoon of the mixture in the middle of a wonton skin. Moisten the edges of two adjacent sides with cold water. Fold the wonton diagonally in half to form a triangle. Press the edges together to seal. Place on the prepared baking sheet. Repeat with the remaining wonton skins and filling. (These may be prepared 24 hours in advance and refrigerated until serving time. Return to room temperature before baking.)

4. Brush the wontons with olive oil.

5. Bake for 10 minutes until puffed and the edges are browned. Serve at once.

6 to 8 portions

SWEET POTATO PILLOWS

NOTATIONS

Wonton skins are plump with a sweet potato purée that's spiked with chipotle chili powder. Baked to a turn instead of fried, these pillows are hot! You can temper the flavor by using regular chili powder if your palate prefers a milder taste.

3/4 pound sweet potato
2 tablespoons mascarpone cheese
1/2 teaspoon chipotle chili powder
salt and freshly ground pepper to taste
24 wonton wraps
PAM or other cooking oil spray

1. Preheat the oven to 400°.

2. Using a fork, prick the potato on all sides. Place the potato directly on the oven rack and bake for 1 hour until tender. Let cool, then peel off the skin. Chop the flesh, put it into the bowl of a food processor, and purée.

3. Grease a large baking sheet.

4. Measure 3/4 cup of purée and place in a bowl. (Reserve the rest of the purée.) Add the mascarpone, chili powder, salt, and pepper and mix well until evenly combined.

5. Place 6 of the wonton wraps on a cutting board. Place 1 tablespoon of the mixture in the middle of each wonton. Moisten the edges with water. Cover the filling with another wonton, pressing gently around the edges to seal. Repeat with the remaining wontons and filling.

6. Place the pillows on the prepared baking sheet. (This may be prepared 24 hours in advance, covered well with plastic wrap, and refrigerated; return to room temperature before baking.) Spray the wontons with PAM.

7. Bake for 10 to 12 minutes until golden. Serve at once.

12 pillows; 6 portions

PORK DUMPLINGS

NOTATIONS

These steamed wonton dumplings are plump with a ground pork filling that's scented with ginger, garlic, and sesame oil. Served with a sesame-soy sauce, they're sure to excite your taste buds.

3/4 pound ground pork
1 large clove garlic, crushed
1 1/2 tablespoons grated gingerroot
2 tablespoons thinly sliced scallion
freshly ground pepper to taste
1 tablespoon soy sauce
1 tablespoon mirin (rice wine)
1 teaspoon sesame oil
27 wonton wraps
Sesame-Soy Sauce (recipe follows)

1. Line a steamer basket with parchment paper.

2. In a bowl, combine the pork, garlic, ginger, scallion, pepper, soy, mirin, and sesame oil and mix until evenly combined.

3. Place 1 tablespoon of the mixture in the middle of each wonton. Moisten the corners with water. Bring the corners up to the middle to form a peak, pinching them together to seal.

4. Place the dumplings in the steamer. Steam for 7 minutes until soft and cooked through. Serve at once with the sesame-soy sauce.

27 dumplings; 9 to 10 portions

Sesame-Soy Sauce:
2 tablespoons soy sauce
2 tablespoons mirin
1/2 teaspoon sesame oil

Combine all of the ingredients and mix well. Set aside until needed.

TOASTED PEANUT BUTTER AND JELLY SANDWICHES

NOTATIONS

These grilled tea sandwiches strut a peanut butter, cream cheese, and jelly filling. Served warm, they're the best pb and j squares this side of heaven.

4 slices hearty white sandwich bread, crusts trimmed
1/4 cup creamy peanut butter
3 tablespoons cream cheese, at room temperature
2 tablespoons raspberry preserves
4 tablespoons butter, at room temperature

1. Spread 2 tablespoons of peanut butter on each of 2 slices of bread. Set aside.

2. Spread 1 1/2 tablespoons of cream cheese on each of the remaining 2 slices of bread. Cover each layer of cream cheese with 1 tablespoon of preserves. Assemble the sandwiches—top the preserves with the peanut butter side of the reserved bread slices.

3. Spread the top of each sandwich with about 1 tablespoon of butter. Cut each sandwich diagonally into quarters.

4. Heat the remaining butter in a non-stick skillet. When hot, add the sandwich triangles, butter side up, to the pan. Sauté until golden on each side, about 2 minutes. Remove to a platter and serve warm.

4 portions

NOTATIONS

BLUE CHEESE-SPINACH STRATA

A strata or bread pudding is real comfort food. This egg custard is abundant with flavor—pungent blue cheese, smoky bacon, zesty red onion, and spinach. Baked until puffed and golden, it can be enjoyed as an appetizer, as a luncheon dish, or for Sunday brunch.

1/2 pound French bread, cut into 1-inch cubes
5 eggs, beaten
2 1/2 cups whole milk
2 tablespoons unsalted butter, melted and cooled
salt and freshly ground pepper to taste
9 to 10-ounce package frozen chopped spinach, thawed and squeezed of its excess liquid
1 cup chopped red onion
6 slices bacon, cooked and chopped
1/2 pound blue cheese, crumbled

1. Preheat the oven to 350°. Grease a 9 x 13-inch baking dish.

2. Put the bread cubes in a large bowl.

3. In a separate bowl, whisk together the eggs, milk, butter, salt, and pepper. Pour the custard over the bread and mix well. Let sit at room temperature for 30 minutes so that the bread can absorb the custard.

4. Add the spinach, onion, bacon, and blue cheese and mix until evenly combined. Turn into the prepared pan.

5. Bake for 40 to 45 minutes until puffed and golden. Cut into squares and serve.

10 to 12 portions

SMALL BITES

NOTATIONS

APPLE, MANCHEGO, AND MEMBRILLO NAPOLEONS

Cheese and fruit are a classic pairing. This easy to prepare appetizer showcases apple slices stacked with Manchego, a hard, slightly sharp, full-flavored Spanish cheese, and topped with membrillo, or quince paste. I like to use both red and green apples for their color and flavor. Visually enticing, these Napoleons make a tantalizing meal opener.

2 apples (1 Granny Smith; 1 McIntosh), cored
1/2 pound Manchego cheese, sliced into 16 pieces
6 ounces membrillo, cut into 16 pieces

1. Slice each apple into 8 rounds.

2. Stack a piece of cheese atop each apple slice. Cap each with a piece of membrillo and serve.

5 to 6 portions

APRICOTS ST. GERMAIN

NOTATIONS

This recipe is one degree of separation from Dates Marais in my ***All-Occasion Cookbook***, and is even more savory. Candied ginger is tucked inside each apricot, giving these bacon-wrapped morsels an unexpected flavor thrill.

24 large dried apricots, sliced almost in half
6 slices candied, crystallized ginger, each cut into 4 strips
8 slices bacon, cut into thirds
dark brown sugar for coating

1. Preheat the oven to 375°. Line a baking sheet with foil and grease the foil.

2. Stuff each apricot with a piece of candied ginger and close tightly.

3. Wrap each apricot with a piece of bacon and secure with a toothpick.

4. Dip both sides of the bacon in brown sugar, pressing gently to help sugar to adhere. Place on the prepared baking sheet.

5. Bake for 10 minutes, turn the apricots over, and bake for 5 to 10 minutes more until browned and glazed. Remove to a plate and serve.

8 portions

NOTATIONS

APRICOTS DE BLEU

Dried apricots are plump with a tangy blue cheese filling and dusted with toasted walnuts. Blue cheese and walnuts are a natural pairing, making these apricots a delectable, pop-in-the-mouth treat.

1/4 cup cream cheese, at room temperature
1/4 cup crumbled blue cheese (Maytag Blue is my personal favorite.)
24 large dried apricots, sliced almost in half
about 3 tablespoons finely chopped walnuts, toasted

1. In a bowl, mix the cream cheese and blue cheese until evenly combined.

2. Stuff each apricot with 1 teaspoon of the mixture. Gently close together. Dip the exposed cheese in the chopped walnuts, coating completely.

3. Serve at room temperature. (These may be made up to 24 hours in advance and refrigerated until needed. Return to room temperature before presenting.)

8 portions

BEET PANCAKES

NOTATIONS

The humble beet makes an Oscar-winning presentation in these crisp, orange-scented pancakes. Complete with a chèvre-horseradish sauce, this is a hard act to follow.

1 pound beets, peeled and coarsely grated
1 medium-size red onion, coarsely grated
1 tablespoon grated orange zest
salt and freshly ground pepper to taste
6 tablespoons all-purpose flour
2 eggs, beaten
6 tablespoons olive oil (not extra-virgin)
Chèvre-Horseradish Sauce (recipe follows)

1. In a bowl, combine the beets, onion, orange zest, salt, and pepper and mix well. Sprinkle the flour over the vegetables and mix until evenly blended.

2. Add the eggs and mix well.

3. Heat 3 tablespoons of the oil in a large skillet. Drop large spoonfuls of the batter into the pan, forming 3-inch rounds. Fry the pancakes over medium heat until brown and crisp on both sides. Remove to a platter and keep warm in a low oven. Repeat with the remaining oil and batter. Serve hot with the chèvre-horseradish sauce.

14 pancakes; 6 to 8 portions

Chèvre-Horseradish Sauce:
3/4 cup sour cream
3 ounces chèvre, crumbled
2 tablespoon prepared white horseradish

Combine all of the ingredients and mix well. Refrigerate until needed.

COUSCOUS CAKES

NOTATIONS

Crispy on the outside and tender on the inside, these plump couscous-laden cakes are resplendent with lemon, pine nuts, and Parmesan. They're the perfect finger food paired with cocktails, are an important addition to a meze plate of olives and feta, and make a stellar companion to a Greek salad.

1¼ cups chicken broth
½ teaspoon salt
1 tablespoon extra-virgin olive oil
1 cup instant couscous
3 eggs, beaten
2 teaspoons finely grated lemon zest
1 tablespoon lemon juice
1 large clove garlic, crushed
⅓ cup thinly sliced scallions
3 tablespoons pine nuts, toasted
¼ cup chopped Italian parsley
½ cup finely grated Parmigiano-Reggiano cheese
6 tablespoons olive oil (not extra-virgin)

1. In a medium-size saucepan, bring the chicken broth, salt, and 1 tablespoon extra-virgin olive oil to a boil. Stir in the couscous, cover, remove from the heat, and let sit for 5 minutes. Fluff with a fork, cover, and let cool completely.

2. Add the eggs, lemon zest, lemon juice, garlic, scallions, pine nuts, parsley, and Parmesan. Mix well until evenly blended.

3. With moistened hands, using ¼ cup of the mixture, form into cakes. Refrigerate for at least 1 hour and up to 24 hours.

4. When ready to serve, heat 2 to 3 tablespoons of oil in a large non-stick skillet. Put half of the cakes in the hot oil and sauté over medium-high heat until golden, about 2 to 3 minutes per side. Remove to a platter and keep warm in a low oven. Repeat with the remaining oil and cakes. Serve hot or warm.

14 cakes; 6 to 8 portions

CUCUMBER BRUSCHETTA

NOTATIONS

This colorful finger food showcases slices of cucumber slathered with cream cheese, topped with smoked salmon, and crowned with a sweet red onion jam.

1 English cucumber
4 ounces cream cheese, at room temperature
2 teaspoons finely chopped dill
3 to 4 ounces smoked salmon, each slice cut into thirds
1/4 cup Red Onion Jam (recipe follows)

1. Trim the ends of the cucumber at an oblique angle. Slice the cucumber on the diagonal into 12 oval slices, each 1/2-inch thick and about 3 inches long.

2. In a bowl, mix the cream cheese and dill, stirring until evenly blended.

3. Spread equal amounts of cream cheese on the cucumber slices. Top each with a piece of smoked salmon. Garnish each bruschetta with 1 teaspoon of red onion jam. Serve at room temperature.

12 bruschetta; 4 to 6 portions

Red Onion Jam:
1 tablespoon olive oil (not extra-virgin)
1 1/4 pounds red onions, halved and thinly sliced
salt to taste
3 tablespoons sugar
1/2 cup red wine vinegar

1. In a large non-stick skillet, heat the oil. Add the onions and season with salt. Cook over medium-high heat for 5 minutes, stirring occasionally. Reduce the heat to low and cook for 20 minutes, stirring occasionally until the onions are golden brown and reduced in volume.

2. Sprinkle with the sugar and add the vinegar. Bring the mixture to a boil and cook for 20 minutes, stirring often. The mixture will develop a thick jam-like consistency. Remove from the heat and let cool to room temperature before using. Store in the refrigerator in a tightly sealed container for up to 3 weeks. The jam is also excellent with grilled meats, sausages, chicken, or fish.

1 1/4 cups

NOTATIONS

CUCUMBER CUPS MEDITERRANÉE

Cucumber cups make an ideal vessel for filling. These cups are brimming with a thick red pepper pesto, lush with Mediterranean ingredients—roasted red pepper, feta, Marcona almonds, and garlic. Once sampled, always savored!

2 English cucumbers, ends trimmed
Red Pepper Pesto (recipe follows)

1. Cut each cucumber into 1-inch thick rounds. Scoop out the core part of each cucumber round, being careful not to go all the way through. You want to create a cucumber cup with 1/4-inch thick sides and bottom.

2. Fill each cup with about 1 tablespoon of the red pepper pesto and serve.

about 24 cups; 8 portions

Red Pepper Pesto:
1 large roasted red pepper, chopped
generous 1/3 pound goat's milk feta cheese, crumbled
1/4 cup roasted, salted Marcona almonds, chopped
1 small clove garlic, crushed
salt and freshly ground pepper to taste

Put all of the ingredients in the bowl of a food processor and purée. Remove to a bowl and refrigerate for 2 hours until firm. (This may be prepared up to 2 days in advance and stored in the refrigerator. Return to room temperature before using.)

about 1 1/2 cups

DATES ROGÈRE

Dates make a wonderful vehicle for stuffing. Metjool dates are the plushest dates, making them the variety of choice. They're filled with sausage meat and baked to a turn, creating the perfect balance of sweet and savory.

NOTATIONS

22 Metjool dates
1/2 pound sausages (sweet or hot—whichever you prefer)

1. Preheat the oven to 375°.

2. Slice each date almost in half lengthwise. Remove the pits.

3. Remove the sausage meat from the casing.

4. Stuff each date with 1/2 tablespoon of sausage meat. Press gently to close. Lay the dates in a baking pan so that the filling is on the side of the date. (This may be prepared up to 24 hours in advance and refrigerated. Return to room temperature before baking.)

5. Bake for 15 minutes until the sausage is cooked and brown. Remove to a platter and serve.

6 to 8 portions

JAZZY HARD-BOILED EGGS

NOTATIONS

When company surprises you unexpectedly, you can whip up these "deviled" eggs in under 20 minutes, and be the perfect host or hostess. They're a great finger food for a large gathering and also make a good addition to the lunch box. There are no specific amounts given; make as many eggs as needed for the occasion.

eggs
salt to taste
Old Bay Seasoning

1. Put the eggs in a saucepan and cover with cold water. Bring to a boil, lower the heat, and simmer gently for 10 minutes. Remove the eggs to a bowl of ice. Add cold water to cover and let sit for 5 to 10 minutes until cooled. Remove from the ice bath and shell the eggs. Slice each egg in half lengthwise. Place cut side up on a platter.

2. Season each egg half with salt, sprinkle with Old Bay, and serve. It dosen't get any easier than that!

allow 2 halves per person

WASABI DEVILED EGGS

Wasabi is the spicy Asian horseradish powder that's classically mixed with soy sauce and served alongside sushi. In this presentation, wasabi excites the palate in deviled eggs, turning the ordinary into the extraordinary.

NOTATIONS

6 extra-large eggs, hard-boiled and shelled
3 tablespoons mayonnaise
2 teaspoons soy sauce
1 tablespoon wasabi powder mixed with 1 teaspoon warm water
pickled ginger for garnish

1. Slice each egg in half lengthwise. Remove the yolks to a bowl and mash.

2. In a separate bowl, mix the mayonnaise, soy sauce, and wasabi until evenly combined. Add the mashed yolks and mix well.

3. Heap the mixture into the egg white shells. Top each egg half with a slice of pickled ginger and serve at room temperature.

6 portions

NOTATIONS

EGG SALAD AND ENDIVE

I have fond memories of my grandmother making egg salad for any family occasion. It was her specialty! This version comes very close to her 5-star recipe. Grating the eggs rather than chopping them makes it distinctive both in taste and texture. Once sampled, always favored. This salad also makes an über sandwich filling.

2 extra-large eggs, hard-boiled
1/8 teaspoon salt
1/2 teaspoon prepared yellow mustard
2 tablespoons mayonnaise
12 endive spears
paprika for dusting

1. Coarsely grate the eggs. Add the salt, mustard, and mayonnaise and mix well until evenly blended. (This may be prepared 24 hours in advance and refrigerated. Return to room temperature to serve.)

2. Spoon 1 tablespoon of the egg mixture onto the bottom end of each endive spear. Dust with paprika and serve.

4 to 6 portions

POTATO, BACON, AND BLUE CHEESE FRITTATA

NOTATIONS

Frittatas are actually baked omelets that are sensational for parties. They play host to a variety of fillings, can be made in advance, and baked when the company arrives. This potato, bacon, and blue cheese medley is one of my favorites.

3/4 pound medium-size red-skinned potatoes, halved, then thinly sliced
2 tablespoons olive oil (not extra-virgin)
salt and freshly ground pepper to taste
8 eggs, beaten
1/4 pound thick sliced bacon, cooked, and coarsely chopped
3 ounces blue cheese, crumbled

1. Preheat the oven to 400°. Grease the bottom and sides of a 9-inch square pan.

2. Arrange the potatoes on the bottom of the pan. Drizzle with olive oil and season with salt and pepper.

3. Bake for 20 minutes until the potatoes are slightly tender.

4. Season the eggs with salt and pepper. Stir in the bacon and blue cheese. Pour the mixture over the potatoes.

5. Bake for 15 to 20 minutes until the eggs are puffed and golden. Cut into 16 squares and serve hot, warm, or at room temperature.

5 to 6 portions

FIGS CELESTE

NOTATIONS

This recipe is actually the next generation of Prosciutto-Wrapped Figs in my ***Home Cooking***. The sweet, dried fruit is plump with a maple-pecan-infused chèvre and wrapped in Italian-cured ham. The complementary tastes of sweet and salty are divine.

4 ounces chèvre, crumbled
1 tablespoon pure maple syrup
2 tablespoons finely chopped pecans, toasted
21 to 22 dried Calimyrna figs, stems removed
21 to 22 thin slices of prosciutto

1. In a bowl, combine the chèvre, maple syrup, and pecans and mix until evenly blended.

2. Slice each fig almost in half through the stem end. Stuff each fig with 1/2 tablespoon of the cheese mixture. Press gently to close.

3. Wrap each fig with a slice of prosciutto and secure with a toothpick. Serve at room temperature. (These may be prepared 24 hours in advance and refrigerated. Return to room temperature to serve.)

8 portions

HERB-ROASTED MUSHROOMS

NOTATIONS

Herbs de Provence is an aromatic blend of dried herbs indigenous to Provence, France. The mixture generally includes rosemary, thyme, savory, and lavender. The herbs lend a special quality to these roasted baby bellas that make them sparkle.

1 pound baby bella mushrooms, stems trimmed off
¼ cup extra-virgin olive oil
salt and freshly ground pepper to taste
1¼ teaspoons herbs de Provence

1. Preheat the oven to 400°.

2. Put the mushrooms in a large bowl. Drizzle with the olive oil and toss until evenly coated. Add the salt, pepper, and herbs de Provence and mix well.

3. Place stem side up in a roasting pan. Roast for 15 minutes. Turn the mushrooms over and roast for 10 minutes more.

4. Remove the mushrooms and any pan juices to a bowl. Serve hot, warm, or at room temperature.

4 to 6 portions

MUSHROOMS TERIYAKI

NOTATIONS

Mushrooms are those pop-in-the-mouth nibbles that continue to enchant us. These are infused with the characteristic sweet-soy flavors of teriyaki, creating an earthy, umami-rich experience.

1/4 cup soy sauce
1/4 cup rice vinegar
1/4 cup mirin (rice wine)
1 cup water
1/4 cup dark brown sugar
1 clove garlic, smashed
1 tablespoon grated gingerroot
freshly ground pepper to taste
1 pound mushrooms (baby bellas or cremini), stems trimmed

1. Put the soy, vinegar, mirin, water, brown sugar, garlic, ginger, and pepper in a 2-quart saucepan and mix well.

2. Add the mushrooms. Bring to a boil, lower the heat, and simmer for 30 minutes, stirring occasionally. Remove from the heat and let cool completely.

3. When ready to serve, drain off the liquid and present at room temperature.

6 portions

SAUSAGE-STUFFED MUSHROOMS

NOTATIONS

Mushrooms make the quintessential basket for stuffing. These caps tout a gusty sausage, cheddar, and bread crumb filling that's baked to a turn.

1/2 pound hot Italian sausages, casing removed
1/2 cup grated sharp cheddar cheese
3 tablespoons diced red onion
1/2 cup fresh bread crumbs
24 large mushrooms (1 3/4 to 2-inches in diameter), stems removed

1. Preheat the oven to 400°.

2. Put the sausage meat in a bowl and break it up with a fork. Add the cheese, onion, and bread crumbs and mix well.

3. Fill each mushroom cap with 1 tablespoon of the mixture, mounding it slightly. Place in a baking pan.

4. Bake for 15 minutes until lightly browned. Serve at once.

6 to 8 portions

STUFFED MUSHROOMS ITALIANO

NOTATIONS

Stuffed mushrooms continue to hold a place of importance in the hors d'oeuvre category. This bread crumb stuffing is speckled with Romano cheese, roasted peppers, capers, and pine nuts, and finished with a swirl of pesto. Baked until golden, they'll be gobbled up in no time.

Stuffing:
1 cup fresh French or Italian bread crumbs
1/4 cup finely grated Romano cheese
1/4 cup diced roasted red pepper
1 tablespoon capers
2 tablespoons pine nuts
2 tablespoons chopped Italian parsley
2 tablespoons pesto (See recipe, page 10)
salt and freshly ground pepper to taste
1/4 cup extra-virgin olive oil

24 white or cremini mushrooms (about 1 3/4-inches in diameter), stems removed

1. Preheat the oven to 400°.

2. In a bowl, combine all of the stuffing ingredients and mix until evenly combined.

3. Fill each mushroom cap with approximately 1/2 tablespoon of the stuffing, pressing the filling into the cavity of each cap. Place the filled caps in a baking pan. (This may be prepared up to 24 hours in advance and refrigerated; return to room temperature before baking.)

4. Bake for 15 to 18 minutes until browned. Serve hot out of the oven. (The mushrooms exude juices during baking which should be discarded.)

8 portions

ROASTED GREEN OLIVES

NOTATIONS

These mouth-watering, tangy green olives are roasted to a turn and then dressed with a fragrant, herbal coating. They make a wonderful accompaniment to a glass of white wine, as well as a perfect enhancement to an antipasto plate.

3 cups large, brine-cured green olives with pits
1 tablespoon extra-virgin olive oil
1 teaspoon grated lemon zest
1 tablespoon lemon juice
1 large clove garlic, smashed
1 teaspoon herbs de Provence

1. Preheat the oven to 400°. Line a baking sheet with foil.

2. Spread the olives out in a single layer on the baking sheet. Roast for 25 minutes. Remove to a bowl.

3. While the olives are roasting, combine the olive oil, lemon zest, lemon juice, garlic, and herbs and mix well.

4. Pour the dressing over the warm olives and mix well.

5. Serve warm or let the olives marinate overnight in the refrigerator and as much as 2 weeks. Return to room temperature to serve.

8 or more portions

ROASTED KALAMATAS

NOTATIONS

The lusty, Italian olive is roasted, concentrating its briny flavor. These cocktail nibbles are absolutely addictive. They also make a welcome addition to salads and pasta dishes. I always have a batch on hand in the refrigerator.

3 cups Kalamata olives with pits
1 tablespoon extra-virgin olive oil
1 tablespoon orange juice
1 large clove garlic, smashed
1/4 teaspoon crushed red pepper flakes (optional)

1. Preheat the oven to 400°. Line a baking sheet with foil.

2. Spread the olives out in a single layer on the baking sheet. Roast for 25 minutes. Remove to a bowl.

3. While the olives are roasting, combine the olive oil, orange juice, garlic, and red pepper flakes and mix well.

4. Pour the oil mixture over the warm olives and mix well until evenly coated.

5. Serve warm or let marinate overnight in the refrigerator and as much as 2 weeks. Return to room temperature to serve with chilled glasses of white wine.

8 or more portions

POLENTA FRIES

NOTATIONS

If you like French fries, you're guaranteed to become enamored with these cornmeal-based sticks that are accented with zesty Romano cheese. Baked until crisp and golden instead of deep-fried, these healthy fries are addictive!

3/4 cup cornmeal
3 3/4 cups water
1/2 teaspoon salt
1 tablespoon butter
PAM or other cooking oil spray
1/2 cup finely grated Romano cheese
3 tablespoons olive oil (not extra-virgin)
sea salt to taste

1. Preheat the oven 325°.

2. Mix the cornmeal with 3/4 cup of cold water, stirring well.

3. In an oven-proof saucepan, combine the 3 cups of water, 1/2 teaspoon salt, and butter. Bring to a boil. Add the cornmeal in a slow, steady stream, stirring constantly until completely incorporated and the mixture begins to thicken slightly. Cover, place in the oven, and bake for 20 minutes.

4. While the polenta is cooking, line a 9 x 13-inch pan with foil, letting the foil overhang both ends. Spray the foil with PAM.

5. When the polenta is cooked, remove it from the oven. Stir in the cheese.

6. Pour the mixture into the prepared pan, spreading it evenly. Let cool; then refrigerate for 2 hours (and as much as 24 hours) until firm.

7. Preheat the oven to 400°. Grease a large baking sheet.

8. Using the foil overhang lift the polenta from the baking pan. Return to room temperature; then cut the polenta in half lengthwise. Cut each half into 3/8-inch wide fingers. Place on the prepared baking sheet. Drizzle with the olive oil.

9. Bake for 40 minutes. Turn over and bake for 10 to 15 minutes more until golden and crisp. Sprinkle with sea salt and serve at once.

6 to 8 portions

PALOMAS

NOTATIONS

I've entitled this recipe palomas, which are actually mini Italian antipasti on individual skewers. Salami, cheese, olives, and Tuscan peppers shine in this fun to eat appetizer.

16 (12-inch long) bamboo skewers
16 queen-size Manzanilla olives (pimiento-stuffed green olives)
16 peperoncini (Tuscan peppers)
16 slices Genoa salami, folded in half, then in quarters
½ pound provolone cheese, cut into 16 cubes (about 1-inch pieces)
2 roasted red peppers, cut into 1 x 2-inch pieces and folded in half (You'll need 16 pieces.)
16 pitted Kalamata olives
16 grape tomatoes

1. Thread each skewer in the following order. Start with a Manzanilla olive to anchor the ingredients. (I like to place the olive in the middle of the skewer, thus leaving a long handle.) Follow with:

peperoncini
quartered salami slice
cheese cube
roasted pepper
Kalamata olive
grape tomato, to cap off the skewer

2. Serve at room temperature. (These may be made up to 24 hours in advance and refrigerated. Return to room temperature to serve.)

16 skewers; 8 portions

POBLANO CHILIES

This is a twist on the popular chilies relleños, or stuffed chili peppers, which is a mainstay of Mexican cuisine. This updated version is baked rather than fried, making it a healthier, but just as delicious dish.

6 large poblano peppers
½ pound crabmeat
4 ounces Boursin cheese
3 to 4 tablespoons olive oil (not extra-virgin)
½ cup panko

1. Remove the stems from the peppers. Scrape out the seeds.

2. Broil the peppers until charred on all sides. Let cool and then peel off the skins.

3. In a bowl, combine the crabmeat and Boursin and mix until evenly blended.

4. Stuff each chili with the crab mixture, pushing the filling down into the cavity of the pepper toward the tip. Secure the top with a toothpick.

5. Preheat the oven to 400°. Grease a baking sheet.

6. Brush each pepper with oil; then roll in the panko to coat completely. Place on the prepared baking sheet.

7. Bake for 15 minutes until crisp and the cheese is oozing. Serve at once.

6 portions

NOTATIONS

NOTATIONS

POPPERS

For those who like it hot—jalapeño peppers are stuffed with a trio of cheeses and baked to a turn. If you want to raise the heat index, don't remove all of the seeds or membranes from the peppers; you'll definitely feel the burn!!!

12 large jalapeño peppers, stems trimmed
4 ounces cream cheese, at room temperature
1/2 cup shredded sharp cheddar cheese
1/2 cup shredded Pepper Jack cheese
2 tablespoons diced red onion

1. Preheat the oven to 400°.

2. Slice the jalapeños in half lengthwise through the stem end. Remove the seeds and ribs.

3. In a bowl, combine the cheeses and red onion and mix until evenly blended.

4. Fill each pepper half with the cheese mixture. Place on a baking sheet.

5. Bake for 18 to 20 minutes until browned and bubbly. Serve at once.

6 to 8 portions

POTATOES OTTO

NOTATIONS

Everybody loves potato nuggets, especially when they're crispy on the outside and tender on the inside. These bite-size taters are roasted to a turn, then served with a yummy, bacon, scallion, and sour cream dipping sauce.

1½ pounds baby red-skinned or fingerling potatoes, cut into 1-inch chunks
2 tablespoons extra-virgin olive oil
sea salt to taste
Bacon-Scallion Sauce (recipe follows)

1. Preheat the oven to 400°.

2. Spread the potato chunks out in a single layer on a rimmed baking sheet. Drizzle with the olive oil, tossing to coat evenly. Sprinkle liberally with the salt.

3. Roast in the oven for 40 minutes, turning the potatoes after 20 minutes. Remove the potatoes to a platter and serve hot, warm, or at room temperature with the dipping sauce.

6 portions

Bacon-Scallion Sauce:
1 cup sour cream
3 tablespoons thinly sliced scallions
4 slices cooked bacon, crumbled

Combine all of the ingredients and mix well. Refrigerate until needed.

Other sauce options may include:

- Sour cream and horseradish
- Mustard mayonnaise
- Barbecue sauce
- Sour cream, grated cheddar, and bacon
- Garlic aioli
- Chili-spiced mayonnaise
- Sour cream and caviar

LACQUERED SALAMI

NOTATIONS

Brown sugar forms a crispy, candy-like glaze on thin slices of Italian salami. These are the perfect finger food with designer martinis.

1/4 pound thinly sliced Genoa salami
about 6 tablespoons dark brown sugar

1. Preheat the oven to 400°. Line a large baking sheet with parchment paper.

2. Lay the salami out in a single layer on the prepared baking sheet. Sprinkle each round with 1 teaspoon of sugar, spreading the sugar evenly with the back of a spoon.

3. Bake for 5 to 6 minutes until browned around the edges. Immediately remove the parchment paper with the salami to a rack to cool. Let sit for 5 minutes; the salami will crisp as it cools. Remove to a platter and serve.

4 to 6 portions

SALAMI CRISPS

Salami and cheese have a natural affinity. Thin slices of Genoa salami are topped with Parmigiano-Reggiano, the infamous Italian cheese which boasts a sweet, nutty taste. Baked to a turn, these crisps rock with flavor.

NOTATIONS

12 thinly sliced rounds of Genoa salami
¾ cup coarsely grated Parmigiano-Reggiano cheese

1. Preheat the oven to 400°. Line two baking sheets with foil.

2. Lay the salami out in a single layer on the prepared baking sheets. Sprinkle each round with 1 tablespoon of cheese.

3. Bake for 9 to 10 minutes until the cheese is lightly golden. Remove to a rack to cool for 1 minute. The melts will crisp as they cool.

4. Place the crisps on a platter and serve.

4 to 6 portions

STUFFED ROMA TOMATOES

NOTATIONS

Roma, or more commonly, plum tomatoes, provide the perfect nest for stuffing. This recipe far exceeds the genre of the proverbial "stuffed tomato". In a class by itself, the dynamic flavor partnering of smoky bacon with the sharp tang of cheddar cheese makes these the ultimate stuffed fruit.

4 plump Roma tomatoes, cut in half through the core

Stuffing:
1/2 cup fresh bread crumbs
1/2 cup coarsely grated sharp cheddar cheese
2 slices bacon, cooked and chopped
salt to taste
3 tablespoons olive oil (not extra-virgin)

1. Preheat the oven to 400°.

2. Using a teaspoon, scoop out the seeds and pulp of each tomato half, leaving a thick shell. Place the tomatoes cut side down on a paper towel to drain for 15 minutes.

3. In a bowl, combine all of the stuffing ingredients, stirring until evenly mixed. (The stuffing may be prepared 24 hours in advance and refrigerated; return to room temperature before proceeding.)

4. Mound the filling in each tomato shell. Place the stuffed tomatoes on a baking sheet.

5. Bake for 20 minutes until golden. Let cool slightly before serving. They're also delicious eaten at room temperature.

4 portions

MEAT AND CHICKEN TIDBITS

STEAK KEBOBS WITH PESTO-MARINARA

NOTATIONS

All you beef lovers take heed! These steak kebobs are grilled to a turn, then served up with a lavish marinara sauce that's swirled with pesto. It's lip-smacking good and totally indulgent. This is also spectacular with grilled chicken, veal chops, shrimp, or pasta.

1¼ to 1½ pounds sirloin tip strip steak, cut into 2-inch cubes
extra-virgin olive oil
salt and freshly ground pepper to taste
Pesto-Marinara Sauce (recipe follows)

1. Skewer the beef cubes. Brush the meat with oil and season with salt and pepper.

2. Grill over hot coals, about 3 minutes per side for medium-rare. Serve with the pesto-marinara sauce.

6 to 8 portions

Pesto-Marinara Sauce:
1 tablespoon extra-virgin olive oil
1 large clove garlic, crushed
1 cup chunky-style, crushed canned tomatoes
1 tablespoon chopped Italian parsley
salt and freshly ground pepper to taste
¼ cup dry red wine
2 tablespoons pesto (see recipe page 10)

1. Heat the oil in a small saucepan. Add the garlic and cook for 1 minute.

2. Add the tomatoes, parsley, salt, pepper, and wine. Bring to a boil, lower the heat, and simmer for 20 minutes uncovered. Remove from the heat.

3. Stir in the pesto and serve with the grilled meat.

1 cup sauce

MEATBALLS MARINARA

NOTATIONS

Meatballs with red sauce continue to be an Italian staple. These much adored nuggets are teeming with spinach, Parmesan, and Port wine, making them a mouth-watering experience. This is a definite crowd-pleaser!

2 eggs, beaten
2 cloves garlic, crushed
1/3 cup diced sweet onion
9 to 10-ounce package frozen, chopped spinach, thawed and squeezed of its excess liquid
3/4 cup fresh bread crumbs
1/2 cup finely grated Parmigiano-Reggiano cheese
1/4 cup chopped Italian parsley
3/4 cup Tawny Port wine
3/4 pound ground veal, broken up
3/4 pound ground pork, broken up
salt and freshly ground pepper to taste
Marinara Sauce (recipe follows)

1. Preheat the oven to 350°. Grease two baking sheets.

2. In a large bowl, combine the eggs, garlic, onion, spinach, bread crumbs, cheese, parsley, and wine and mix well.

3. Add the veal and pork. Season with salt and pepper. Gently mix the meat into the spinach and cheese mixture, being careful not to over mix the meat—this helps to insure tender meatballs.

4. With moistened hands, using 2 tablespoons of the mixture, form into golf ball size nuggets, being careful not to pack the meat tightly. Place on the prepared baking sheets, 1 1/2 inches apart.

5. Bake for 10 minutes. Remove from the oven, add the meatballs to the marinara sauce, heat gently for 5 to 10 minutes covered, and serve at once.

3 dozen meatballs; 10 to 12 portions

NOTATIONS

Marinara Sauce:
3 tablespoons extra-virgin olive oil
1 large clove garlic, crushed
28-ounce can crushed Italian tomatoes
1 teaspoon dried basil
1/4 cup chopped Italian parsley
salt and freshly ground pepper to taste

1. In a large saucepan, warm the oil. Add the garlic and sauté for 1 minute.

2. Add the remaining ingredients. Bring to a boil, cover, lower the heat, and simmer for 20 minutes. (This may be prepared up to 24 hours in advance and stored in the refrigerator. Reheat before proceeding.)

STUFFED CABBAGE ROLLS

NOTATIONS

My grandmother made the all-time best sweet and sour cabbage. This stream-lined version showcases neat packages of meat-filled cabbage bundles that are bathed in her delectable sauce. I instruct you to freeze the cabbage and then defrost it—this process softens the cabbage leaves, eliminating the need to boil them.

2 eggs, beaten
1 medium-size onion, finely diced
1¼ cups fresh bread crumbs
½ cup Ruby Port wine
2 pounds ground sirloin, broken up
salt and freshly ground pepper to taste
1 large head Savoy cabbage, frozen and then thawed
Sweet-Sour Sauce (recipe follows)

1. Preheat the oven to 350°. Grease a large baking dish.

2. In a large bowl, combine the eggs, onion, bread crumbs, and wine and mix well.

3. Add the ground sirloin. Season with salt and pepper. Gently mix the meat into the bread crumb mixture, being careful not to over mix the meat.

4. Separate the cabbage leaves from the core.

5. Place ½ cup of the meat mixture in the middle of each cabbage leaf. Fold up the core end to cover the filling. Fold in the left and right sides to enclose the ends; then finish rolling up the cabbage.

6. Place seam side down in the prepared baking pan. Cover with the sweet-sour sauce. (This may be prepared 24 hours in advance and refrigerated; return to room temperature before cooking.)

7. Cover the pan and bake for 1 hour. Uncover, baste with the sauce, and bake for 30 minutes more, basting after 15 minutes. Serve piping hot.

11 to 12 cabbage bundles; 11 to 12 portions

NOTATIONS

Sweet-Sour Sauce:
28-ounce can crushed tomatoes
1/2 cup dark brown sugar
1/4 cup lemon juice
1/2 cup Ruby Port wine
1/2 teaspoon ground ginger
1/2 cup golden raisins
salt to taste

In a bowl, combine all of the ingredients and mix well. Set aside until needed.

PORK BALLS IN LETTUCE POCKETS

NOTATIONS

These fluffy, mouth-watering meatballs are teeming with Asian flavors—ginger, garlic, scallions, and shiitake mushrooms. After being baked to a turn, they are sauced with a honey-hoisin glaze and presented in lettuce cups.

2 eggs, beaten
1/2 cup mirin (rice wine)
3/4 cup panko
1 1/2 tablespoons soy sauce
salt and freshly ground pepper to taste
2 cloves garlic, crushed
2 tablespoons finely grated gingerroot
1/4 cup thinly sliced scallions
3/4 cup finely diced shiitake mushroom caps
1 1/2 pounds ground pork
Boston lettuce leaves
Hoisin Glaze (recipe follows)

1. Preheat the oven to 350°. Grease two baking sheets.

2. In a large bowl, combine the eggs, mirin, panko, soy, salt, pepper, garlic, gingerroot, scallions, and mushrooms and mix well.

3. Add the pork and mix until evenly combined.

4. With moistened hands, using 2 tablespoons of the mixture, form into golf ball size nuggets. Place on the prepared baking sheets, 1 1/2-inches apart.

5. Bake for 10 minutes. Remove from the oven. Place each meatball in a lettuce leaf, spoon the glaze over the nuggets, and serve warm.

30 meatballs; 10 to 12 portions

Hoisin Glaze:
3 tablespoons hoisin sauce
1 tablespoon honey
6 tablespoons mirin

Combine all of the ingredients in a small saucepan. Bring to a boil, lower the heat, and simmer for 2 to 3 minutes. (This may be made 24 hours in advance and stored in the refrigerator; reheat before using.)

NOTATIONS

GRILLED SAUSAGES WITH MANGO MUSTARD

This hors d'oeuvre is all about the mustard. The condiment is a savory blend of yellow mustard and puréed mango with chili, cumin, and curry. The mustard is both spicy and seductive. Try it also with grilled shrimp, chicken, or burgers.

Mango Mustard:
1 cup prepared yellow mustard (French's is a good choice.)
1 cup puréed mango (fresh or frozen)
1/4 cup packed dark brown sugar
1 tablespoon curry powder
1 tablespoon chili powder
1 tablespoon ground cumin
1/8 teaspoon cayenne pepper
salt and freshly ground pepper to taste

Put all of the mustard ingredients in a bowl and mix well. Refrigerate until needed. This will keep for 3 weeks—the recipe makes more than what you'll need.

about 2 1/2 cups

1 pound sweet or hot sausages
olive oil (not extra-virgin)

1. Rub the sausages with olive oil. Grill for 4 to 5 minutes per side until cooked and browned. Cut into 1-inch chunks.

2. Serve the sausage chunks with the mango mustard as a dipping sauce.

6 portions

LAMB LOLLYPOPS

NOTATIONS

These baby lamb chops from the rack are encrusted with a brown sugar-mustard coating. Glazed and oozing with mouth-watering flavor, this is definite party fare.

2 racks of lamb, trimmed
salt and freshly ground pepper to taste
1/4 cup dark brown sugar
2 tablespoons dry mustard
2 tablespoons Dijon mustard

1. Preheat the oven to 450°.

2. Season the racks of lamb on all sides with salt and pepper.

3. In a small bowl, combine the brown sugar and mustards, mixing until evenly combined. Spread the mixture on all surfaces of the racks of lamb. Set the racks in a roasting pan, meat side up.

4. Roast for 20 minutes for rare; 25 minutes for medium-rare. Let the meat rest for 5 minutes; then slice into individual chops and serve.

16 lollypops; 8 portions

GLAZED CHICKEN WINGS

NOTATIONS

Chicken wings rank as a number one favorite finger food. Crisp and delish, these little darlings are coated with a balsamic-apricot jam and baked to a turn. Guaranteed you'll keep coming back for more.

2¼ pounds chicken wings, wing tips removed (10 to 12 wings)
½ cup apricot preserves
2 tablespoons balsamic vinegar
salt and freshly ground pepper to taste

1. Preheat the oven to 400°. Grease a large baking pan.

2. Cut the chicken wings in half, separating the drumsticks from the wingettes. Put the pieces in a large bowl.

3. In a separate bowl, combine the preserves, vinegar, salt, and pepper. Pour the mixture over the chicken and mix well until evenly coated. Place the wings skin side up in the prepared baking pan, coating with any extra sauce.

4. Bake for 45 to 50 minutes until crisp and bronze. Remove to a platter and serve hot, warm, or at room temperature.

6 portions

CHICKEN WINGS TERIYAKI

NOTATIONS

Chicken wings lend themselves to a host of presentations. This Asian-style finger food sports a caramelized brown sugar-soy glaze that's lip-smacking good. The teriyaki marinade is also great over grilled tuna, salmon, or steak.

1½ pounds chicken wings, wing tips removed
¼ cup dark brown sugar
2 tablespoons soy sauce
freshly ground pepper to taste
2 tablespoons coarsely grated gingerroot
1 large clove garlic, crushed
2 tablespoons mirin (rice wine)

1. Cut the chicken wings in half, separating the drumsticks from the wingettes. Put the pieces in a large bowl.

2. In a separate small bowl, combine the brown sugar, soy, pepper, ginger, garlic, and mirin and mix well.

3. Pour the marinade over the chicken pieces and let marinate at least 1 hour in the refrigerator and as much as overnight. Return to room temperature before proceeding.

4. Preheat the oven to 400°. Grease a large roasting pan.

5. Place the chicken skin side up in the prepared pan along with any of the marinade.

6. Roast for 40 minutes until golden and glazed, basting with the pan juices after 20 minutes. Baste once more before removing to a platter to serve. Enjoy hot, warm, or at room temperature.

4 to 6 portions

PROSCIUTTO-WRAPPED CHICKEN

NOTATIONS

Chicken and prosciutto are a classic Italian combination. The salty, dry-cured ham lends a distinctive quality and exquisite flavor to the chicken. Chicken tenders are first marinated in a lush orange-balsamic vinaigrette, then wrapped with sliced prosciutto, and grilled to a turn. Delish!

salt and freshly ground pepper to taste
1 large clove garlic, crushed
1 teaspoon Dijon mustard
2 tablespoons orange marmalade
1/4 cup balsamic vinegar
2 tablespoons extra-virgin olive oil
12 plump chicken tenders
12 thin slices imported prosciutto
12 bamboo skewers, soaked in water for 15 minutes

1. In a bowl, whisk together the salt, pepper, garlic, Dijon, orange marmalade, vinegar, and oil until thick.

2. Pour the vinaigrette over the chicken and refrigerate for 3 to 4 hours to marinate.

3. Remove the chicken from the marinade and reserve the marinade.

4. Wrap each tender with a slice of prosciutto and thread each tender on a separate skewer.

5. Grill the chicken over hot coals about 3 minutes per side, basting with the reserved marinade. The chicken should be cooked and the prosciutto glazed. Present chicken on skewers either warm or at room temperature.

6 to 8 portions

GRILLED RED CURRY CHICKEN TENDERS

NOTATIONS

This red curry and coconut milk marinade is infused with brown sugar, fish sauce, and gingerroot, lending a Malaysian spin to grilled tenders. They're moist, succulent, and bursting with flavor.

½ cup unsweetened coconut milk
1 tablespoon red curry paste
1 tablespoon dark brown sugar
1 teaspoon Asian fish sauce
1 teaspoon finely grated gingerroot
1½ pounds chicken tenders
about 12 bamboo skewers, soaked in water for 15 minutes

1. In a small bowl, mix together the coconut milk, curry paste, brown sugar, fish sauce, and gingerroot until smooth.

2. Put the chicken in a roasting pan in a single layer. Pour the marinade over the chicken, coating both sides. Let marinate for 30 minutes at room temperature.

3. Thread each tender on a separate skewer.

4. Grill the tenders over hot coals, about 2 to 3 minutes per side until cooked and slightly charred. Serve on skewers hot off the grill or let cool to room temperature and present.

6 portions

CHICKEN TENDERS TANDOORI

NOTATIONS

Tandoori is a traditional Indian dish. Typically, chicken is marinated in a mixture of yogurt and aromatic spices, and then cooked in a hot tandoori or clay oven. I've put a slightly different twist on the classic dish. Moist and fragrant, these grilled chicken tenders are special indeed.

Tandoori Marinade:
1 cup plain Greek yogurt
2 large cloves garlic, crushed
1 tablespoon grated gingerroot
1½ teaspoons ground cumin
1½ teaspoons ground coriander
½ teaspoon paprika
¼ to ½ teaspoon crushed red pepper flakes
salt and freshly ground pepper to taste

1½ pounds plump chicken tenders
bamboo skewers, soaked in water for 15 minutes
oil for the grill

1. In a bowl, combine all of the marinade ingredients and mix well.

2. Put the chicken in a roasting pan in a single layer. Pour the marinade over the chicken, spreading it to cover completely. Refrigerate for 4 hours to allow the flavors to blend together.

3. Remove the chicken from the refrigerator and let come to room temperature. Lift the tenders out of the marinade, removing any excess marinade. Thread each tender on a separate skewer.

4. Oil the grill grate. Grill the chicken over hot coals for 2 to 3 minutes per side until cooked and charred. Serve the chicken on skewers.

6 to 8 portions

SEAFOOD MORSELS

DEVILED BLUEFISH PÂTÉ

NOTATIONS

This creamy, zesty bluefish spread is abuzz with Dijon, horseradish, and Worcestershire sauce. I like to serve it with slices of French bread.

1/2 pound skinless, boneless bluefish
olive oil
salt and freshly ground pepper to taste
4 ounces cream cheese, at room temperature
1 tablespoon diced red onion
1/2 tablespoon Dijon mustard
1/2 tablespoon prepared white horseradish
1 tablespoon lemon juice
1/2 teaspoon Worcestershire sauce

1. Preheat the oven to 400°.

2. Rub the bluefish with olive oil and season with salt and pepper. Place in a baking dish.

3. Bake for 10 to 12 minutes until the fish is cooked through. Let cool.

4. Break the fish into chunks and put them and any accumulated juices in the bowl of a food processor. Add the remaining ingredients and season with salt and pepper. Purée the mixture until smooth and creamy.

5. Remove the pâté to a bowl and serve. (This may be prepared up to 24 hours in advance and refrigerated; return to room temperature to serve.)

6 portions

SAUSAGES AND CLAMS

NOTATIONS

We usually see this ever-popular surf and turf pairing in fish stews and pasta dishes. It takes on a totally new personality when grilled. It's served with a zesty horseradish-mustard sauce that will keep you coming back for more.

1 pound chicken or pork sausages (hot or sweet or a combination of both)
1 tablespoon extra-virgin olive oil
36 cherrystone clams, well-rinsed
Horseradish-Mustard Sauce (recipe follows)

1. Rub the sausages with the oil. Grill over hot coals about 10 minutes until cooked and browned. Remove to a platter and cut into 1-inch chunks.

2. Place the clams on the grill and cook until the shells pop open—it should take about 5 minutes. Remove the clams from the grill as they open.

3. Mound the clams on the platter alongside the sausages. Serve warm or at room temperature with the horseradish-mustard sauce.

6 portions

Horseradish-Mustard Sauce:
1/2 cup mayonnaise
2 tablespoons Dijon mustard
1 tablespoon prepared white horseradish
1/4 teaspoon Worcestershire sauce

Combine all of the ingredients and mix well until evenly blended. Refrigerate until needed.

NOTATIONS

CRAB RANGOON REVISITED

This recipe first appeared in my ***All-Occasion Cookbook***. This updated version of the crab-stuffed pillows takes a modern day turn with a distinctive wasabi cream cheese. Ooh la la!

4 ounces crabmeat
4 ounces cream cheese, at room temperature
2 tablespoons thinly sliced scallion
1 tablespoon wasabi powder mixed with 1/2 tablespoon warm water to form a paste
27 wonton wraps
1 1/2 tablespoons olive oil (not extra-virgin)

1. Preheat the oven to 375°. Grease two baking sheets.

2. In a bowl, combine the crabmeat, cream cheese, scallion, and wasabi and mix well.

3. Place 1/2 tablespoon of the mixture in the middle of a wonton wrap. Moisten the edges of two adjacent sides with cold water. Fold the wonton diagonally in half to form a triangle. Press the edges together to seal. Place on the prepared baking sheet. Repeat with the remaining wonton skins and filling. (These may be prepared 24 hours in advance and refrigerated until serving time. Return to room temperature before baking.)

4. Brush the wontons with olive oil.

5. Bake for 10 to 12 minutes until golden. Serve at once.

9 to 10 portions

SHRIMP TOASTS

NOTATIONS

Shrimp toasts are a Chinese appetizer I remember enjoying in my childhood. I have tailored the original fried version of the recipe, making it healthier, easier to prepare, and every bit as delicious.

1/2 pound shelled raw shrimp, finely chopped
1/2 cup finely chopped water chestnuts
1/4 cup thinly sliced scallions
1 teaspoon sugar
salt to taste
1/2 cup mayonnaise
7 slices Pepperidge Farm white sandwich bread
1 cup panko
cooking oil spray

1. Preheat the oven to 400°.

2. In a bowl, combine the shrimp, water chestnuts, scallions, sugar, salt, and mayonnaise and mix well.

3. Spread equal amounts of the mixture on the bread slices. Sprinkle with the panko, coating generously.

4. With a thin, sharp knife, cut each slice of bread diagonally into quarters. Place on a baking sheet. Spray generously with PAM or other cooking oil spray.

5. Bake for 12 to 15 minutes until golden. Serve hot. I like to serve the toasts with duck sauce.

28 squares; 6 to 8 portions

NOTATIONS

SHRIMP WITH CHIPOTLE MAYONNAISE

Shrimp cocktail takes on a new identity when accompanied by this spicy chipotle mayonnaise. I like to roast the shrimp instead of boiling them to enhance their flavor.

1 pound raw shrimp, shelled (16 to 20 count)
extra-virgin olive oil
salt to taste
7-ounce can chipotle peppers in adobo
3/4 cup mayonnaise

1. Preheat the oven to 400°.

2. Put the shrimp on a baking sheet in a single layer. Drizzle with olive oil and season with salt.

3. Roast for 6 to 8 minutes, just until they turn pink and firm. Let cool.

4. Dice 1 chipotle pepper. Put 1 tablespoon of chopped pepper and 1 tablespoon of adobo sauce in a bowl. (Refrigerate the rest for later use.)

5. Add the mayonnaise to the bowl and mix well until evenly combined.

6. Surround the spicy mayonnaise with the roasted shrimp and serve.

6 portions

SHRIMP WITH MANGO SALSA

NOTATIONS

Shrimp are bathed in a classic mango salsa fragrant with cilantro, jalapeño, and lime. This makes a luscious and most colorful presentation. It also works well with grilled scallops.

Mango Salsa:
1 1/2 cups peeled, diced mango (cut into 3/4-inch pieces)
1/2 cup diced red pepper
1 medium-size jalapeño pepper, seeded and diced
1/4 cup diced red onion
2 tablespoons finely chopped cilantro
salt to taste
1 tablespoon honey
2 tablespoons lime juice

1 1/2 pounds poached shrimp, shelled

1. In a mixing bowl, combine all of the salsa ingredients. Let marinate at room temperature for 1 to 2 hours.

2. Put the shrimp in a large bowl. Add the salsa, mix well, and let marinate at room temperature for 30 minutes before serving. (If you want to marinate it longer, refrigerate for up to 8 hours. Return to room temperature to serve.)

6 to 8 portions

NOTATIONS

AVOCADO AND SMOKED SALMON ROLL-UPS

Sushi-like in appearance, these roll-ups feature creamy avocado slices nestled with Boursin cheese and wrapped with smoked salmon. The pairing of the green fruit with the coral-hued fish is both visually vibrant and seductive.

1 Haas avocado, cut in half lengthwise and pitted
8 slices (about 7 to 8 ounces) smoked salmon
3 tablespoons Boursin cheese

1. Using a spoon, carefully scoop the avocado halves from the skin. Slice each avocado half into 4 lengthwise wedges.

2. Place a wedge of avocado at the end of a slice of salmon. Put a full teaspoon of Boursin in the hollow of the avocado. Roll up the salmon, wrapping the avocado inside. Secure the roll with a toothpick. Serve at room temperature with soy sauce mixed with wasabi for dipping.

4 portions

SMOKED SALMON ROLLS

For those who are squeamish about eating raw fish, this sushi-style appetizer is perfect for you. Shrimp are stuffed with a dill-cream cheese and then rolled up in a slice of smoked salmon. This is elegant party fare.

NOTATIONS

16 extra-large shelled shrimp, cooked
4 ounces cream cheese, at room temperature
2 tablespoons finely chopped dill
1 tablespoon chopped chives
8 thin slices smoked salmon (about 7 to 8 ounces)

1. Butterfly each shrimp along the length of the outside edge.

2. In a bowl, combine the cream cheese, dill, and chives and mix until evenly blended.

3. Stuff each shrimp with $1\frac{1}{2}$ teaspoons of the cream cheese mixture. Press together gently.

4. Slice each piece of smoked salmon in half lengthwise. You will have 16 thin strips.

5. Wrap each shrimp with a piece of smoked salmon, secure with a toothpick, and serve. (This may be prepared 3 to 4 hours in advance and refrigerated; return to room temperature to serve.)

6 to 8 portions

NOTATIONS

SMOKED SALMON TARTARE

A tartare is typically chopped raw beef, salmon, or tuna that's highly seasoned. Onions, parsley, capers, and lemon juice are generally the ingredients of choice to enhance the meat or fish. I've taken the concept of tartare one step further and have featured smoked salmon as the key ingredient. The tartare is then presented atop slices of pumpernickel bread. It also dazzles as a topping for pasta or scrambled eggs and as a relish for grilled salmon.

8 ounces smoked salmon, chopped
2 tablespoons diced red onion
2 tablespoons thinly sliced scallion
1 tablespoon capers
2 tablespoons chopped Italian parsley
1 tablespoon finely chopped dill
freshly ground pepper to taste
1½ tablespoons extra-virgin olive oil
6 to 8 slices pumpernickel bread, toasted and cut into quarters

1. Combine the salmon, onion, scallion, capers, parsley, dill, pepper, and oil and mix well. Let sit for 30 minutes to allow flavors to blend.

2. Mound spoonfuls atop the bread toasts and serve.

6 to 8 portions

INTERLUDES

Salads have become a mainstay in American cuisine, whether it's a garden variety, a grain or bean medley, or a hearty main dish. Salad composition is an art, in which you must achieve a balance of the ingredients, textures, and flavors. It should be visually exciting as well as delicious.

Freshness is the key component when creating salads. Greenery and vegetables should be crisp and varied, fruits ripe and sweet, nuts toasted, and cheeses deep-flavored.

I have created a large array of different and interesting salad combinations. Each salad sports its own distinctive dressing designed to enhance those specific ingredients. My personal palette favorites for accents include: olives, pine nuts, pecans, Parmesan, chèvre, Dijon mustard, and roasted peppers. I particularly like to combine fruits—both fresh and dried—with nuts in composed salads.

Let your creativity flow and make salads colorful and imaginative, delighting in the bounty of the harvest.

GARDEN GREENERY

NOTATIONS

APRICOT, BRIE, AND SMOKED ALMOND SALAD

Fragrant dried apricots and smoky almonds have a magnetic attraction. When combined with the buttery richness of Brie cheese, these ingredients sparkle in this lustrous salad of contrasting tastes and textures.

10 ounces mesclun
18 dried apricots, halved
1/4 pound Brie cheese, cut into bite-size pieces
1/3 cup smoked almonds, coarsely chopped

Sherry Vinaigrette:
salt and freshly ground pepper to taste
1 tablespoon apricot preserves
1 1/2 tablespoons sherry vinegar
1/3 cup extra-virgin olive oil

1. Heap the mesclun in a large bowl. Add the apricots, Brie, and almonds.

2. In a separate small bowl, whisk together the salt, pepper, apricot preserves, vinegar, and oil until thick.

3. Pour the vinaigrette over the salad, toss well until evenly coated, and serve at once.

6 portions

ARUGULA-FIG SALAD

NOTATIONS

A derivative of Spinach, Bacon, and Fig Salad in my ***Home Cooking,*** this composition is even more sumptuous. Peppery arugula is crowned with sweet, dried figs, fragrant, toasted pecans, and heady goat cheese and is napped with a yummy, maple-balsamic vinaigrette. This is sure to become a family favorite!

10 ounces baby arugula
15 dried Black Mission figs, stems removed and halved through the stem end
2/3 cup coarsely chopped pecans, toasted
4 ounces chèvre, crumbled

Maple-Balsamic Vinaigrette:
salt and freshly ground pepper to taste
1 medium-size shallot, diced
1 teaspoon Dijon mustard
2 tablespoons pure maple syrup
2 tablespoon balsamic vinegar
6 tablespoons olive oil (not extra-virgin)

1. Heap the arugula in a large bowl. Add the figs and pecans.

2. In a separate small bowl, whisk together the salt, pepper, shallot, Dijon, maple syrup, vinegar, and oil until thick.

3. Pour the vinaigrette over the salad and toss well until evenly coated.

4. Sprinkle with the chèvre and serve at once.

6 portions

NOTATIONS

ARUGULA, GRAPEFRUIT, AND RED ONION SALAD

This trio of ingredients is a refreshing combination. The peppery taste of arugula is offset by the sweet, juicy chunks of grapefruit, and is punctuated with the zip of red onion. The honey-lime vinaigrette is accented with mint and cilantro, making it the perfect counterpoint to the salad.

7 ounces baby arugula
segments from 1 large red grapefruit, cut into bite-size pieces
1/2 medium-size red onion, thinly sliced

Honey-Lime Vinaigrette:
salt and freshly ground pepper to taste
1 tablespoon honey
2 tablespoons finely chopped mint
2 tablespoons finely chopped cilantro
1 1/2 tablespoons lime juice
1/4 cup extra-virgin olive oil

1. Heap the arugula in a large bowl. Add the grapefruit and onion.

2. In a separate small bowl, whisk together the salt, pepper, honey, mint, cilantro, lime juice, and oil.

3. Pour the vinaigrette over the salad, toss gently until evenly mixed, and serve at once.

4 portions

ASIAN-STYLE SHREDDED ROMAINE SALAD

NOTATIONS

Shredded romaine forms the base for this Asian-inspired salad. It's topped with cucumber, scallions, sesame seeds, and edamame, the stylish soy bean. All is covered with a ginger vinaigrette, reflecting the rich flavors of the Far East.

2 hearts romaine, cut into 1/2-inch wide strips
1/2 English cucumber, thinly sliced
1/2 cup shelled edamame, steamed
1/4 cup thinly sliced scallions
4 teaspoons sesame seeds, toasted

Ginger Vinaigrette:
salt and freshly ground pepper to taste
1 clove garlic, smashed
1 tablespoon finely grated gingerroot
1/2 tablespoon Asian fish sauce
2 tablespoons rice vinegar
1 tablespoon toasted sesame oil
1/4 cup olive oil (not extra-virgin)

1. Heap the romaine in a large bowl. Add the cucumber, edamame, scallions, and sesame seeds.

2. In a separate small bowl, whisk together the salt, pepper, garlic, gingerroot, fish sauce, vinegar, sesame oil, and olive oil.

3. When ready to serve, remove the garlic from the dressing. Pour the vinaigrette over the salad, toss well until evenly coated, and present.

4 portions

CHOPPED ASPARAGUS SALAD

NOTATIONS

Although a harbinger of spring, asparagus is no longer a seasonal vegetable and can be enjoyed year round. In this presentation, chopped raw asparagus joins forces with lush Mediterranean ingredients—roasted peppers, pine nuts, raisins, capers, and Parmesan cheese—that will keep you coming back for more. It makes a stellar addition to barbecues, picnics, and buffets.

1 pound pencil-thin asparagus, ends trimmed, cut into 1/2-inch long pieces (If only mature stalks are available, peel them before slicing.)
1 medium-size roasted red pepper, chopped
1/4 cup raisins, plumped in hot water for 2 minutes and drained
1/4 cup pine nuts, toasted
1 tablespoon capers
1/4 cup coarsely grated Parmigiano-Reggiano cheese

Vinaigrette:
salt and freshly ground pepper to taste
1 1/2 teaspoons amber agave nectar
1 1/2 tablespoons sherry vinegar
3 tablespoons extra-virgin olive oil

1. Put the asparagus in a large bowl. Add the roasted pepper, raisins, pine nuts, capers, and Parmesan.

2. In a separate small bowl, whisk together the salt, pepper, agave, vinegar, and oil until thick.

3. Pour the vinaigrette over the salad and toss well until evenly coated. Let marinate for 1 hour at room temperature and present.

4 portions

AVOCADO SALSA-SALAD

The ever-popular avocado is actually a fruit, as it has a pit. Its mild, buttery taste is enlivened with layers of flavor in this jazzed-up dish. Enjoy it as a salsa atop a piece of grilled chicken or savor it as a salad alongside a juicy burger.

NOTATIONS

3 Haas avocados, pitted, peeled, and cut into 1-inch chunks
3 medium-size tomatoes, coarsely chopped
1 English cucumber, cut into bite-size chunks
1/2 medium-size red onion, thinly sliced
toasted tortilla wedges

Cilantro Vinaigrette:
salt and freshly ground pepper to taste
1 clove garlic, minced
1 jalapeño pepper, seeded and diced
1 teaspoon honey
1/4 cup chopped cilantro
generous pinch of cayenne pepper
2 tablespoons lime juice
1/4 cup extra-virgin olive oil

1. Put the avocados in a bowl. Add the tomatoes, cucumber, and red onion.

2. In a separate small bowl, whisk together the salt, pepper, garlic, jalapeño pepper, honey, cilantro, cayenne, lime juice, and oil.

3. Pour the vinaigrette over the salad and mix gently until evenly coated. Serve with toasted tortilla wedges.

6 to 8 portions

NOTATIONS

BABY GREENS WITH POMEGRANATE-MOLASSES VINAIGRETTE

Pomegranate juice is definitely the rage. It's prized for its nutritional value as a heart-healthy drink, rich in anti-oxidants. Its slightly tart flavor adds pizzazz to the dressing, and its seeds add a burst of juicy fruitiness to the composition, making it the hallmark of this dish.

10 ounces baby romaine
1/2 cup pomegranate seeds
1/4 cup pine nuts, toasted

Pomegranate-Molasses Vinaigrette:
2/3 cup pomegranate juice
salt and freshly ground pepper to taste
1 tablespoon molasses
1/4 cup chopped chives
1 tablespoon balsamic vinegar
1/4 cup olive oil (not extra-virgin)

1. Heap the greens in a large bowl. Add the pomegranate seeds and pine nuts.

2. In a small saucepan, heat the pomegranate juice. Bring to a boil, reduce the heat, and simmer about 12 minutes or so until it is reduced to 1/4 cup. Remove from the heat and let cool. (This may be made 24 hours in advance and refrigerated.)

3. In a small bowl, whisk the salt, pepper, reduced pomegranate juice, molasses, chives, vinegar, and oil.

4. Pour the vinaigrette over the salad, toss gently until evenly coated, and serve at once.

4 to 6 portions

FRENCH BY DESIGN

NOTATIONS

Don't let the pure simplicity of the ingredients in this stylish salad fool you. The layers of flavor offer a range of complexity that is divine. Mix greens are sprinkled with sweet raspberries, tangy feta, and nutty pistachios, and then dressed in a vanilla-balsamic vinaigrette.

10 ounces mesclun
1/2 pint raspberries
1/3 cup shelled pistachio nuts
4 ounces goat's milk feta cheese, crumbled

Vanilla-Balsamic Vinaigrette:
salt and freshly ground pepper to taste
1 teaspoon pure vanilla extract
2 tablespoons balsamic vinegar
1/3 cup extra-virgin olive oil

1. Heap the mesclun in a large bowl. Add the raspberries and pistachios.

2. In a separate small bowl, whisk together the salt, pepper, vanilla, vinegar, and oil.

3. Pour the vinaigrette over the salad and toss gently until evenly coated. Sprinkle with the feta and serve at once.

6 portions

BEET, CHÈVRE, AND WALNUT SALAD

NOTATIONS

The dynamic medley of sweet beets, heady goat cheese, and toasted walnuts luxuriates in this savory salad. Napped in a creamy, horseradish dressing, this salad offers layers of flavors.

3/4 pound young beets, trimmed (purple or golden, or a combination)
10 ounces mesclun
1/2 cup chopped walnuts, toasted
4 ounces chèvre, crumbled

Horseradish-Cream:
salt and freshly ground pepper to taste
1 tablespoon white horseradish
1 tablespoon heavy cream
1 tablespoon lemon juice
1/4 cup olive oil (not extra-virgin)

1. Put the beets in a saucepan and add cold water to cover. Bring to a boil, reduce the heat, cover, and simmer for 35 to 45 minutes, just until the beets are tender. Drain and let cool. When cool, slip off the skins and cut the beets into 3/4-inch chunks.

2. Heap the mesclun in a large bowl. Add the beets and walnuts.

3. In a separate small bowl, whisk together the salt, pepper, horseradish, cream, lemon juice, and oil until thick and creamy.

4. Pour the dressing over the salad and toss well. Garnish with the crumbled chèvre and serve at once.

6 portions

BORSCHT SALAD

NOTATIONS

Modeled after the classic cold beet soup, this salad is a stunner. Plump with Russian-style ingredients—chunks of beets, cucumbers, and potatoes—and blanketed in a dill-sour cream sauce, this dish is sure to garner praise. It makes a lovely summer luncheon dish.

1 1/4 pounds young beets, trimmed
1/2 pound medium-size red-skinned potatoes, cut into 3/4-inch cubes
2 cups chopped English cucumber, cut into 3/4-inch cubes
1/2 cup chopped scallions

Dill-Sour Cream:
1 cup sour cream
salt and freshly ground pepper to taste
1 1/2 tablespoons sugar
2 tablespoons chopped dill
3 tablespoons white wine vinegar

1. Put the beets in a saucepan and add cold water to cover. Bring to a boil, reduce the heat, cover, and simmer for 35 to 45 minutes, just until the beets are tender. Drain and let cool. When cool, slip off the skins and cut the beets into 3/4-inch chunks. Transfer to a medium-size bowl.

2. Boil the potatoes in salted water until fork tender, about 10 to 12 minutes. Drain well and let cool.

3. Add the cooled potatoes, cucumber, and scallions to the beets.

4. Put the sour cream in a separate small bowl. Add the salt, pepper, sugar, dill, and vinegar and whisk until smooth.

5. Pour the sauce over the beet salad, mixing until evenly coated, and serve.

6 portions

CAESAR SALAD REVISITED

NOTATIONS

Caesar salad is undoubtedly one of the most favored salads. As of late, it has seen a host of innovative interpretations. This rendition is my all-time favorite. It showcases hearts of romaine blanketed in a creamy mustard-mayonnaise that's perfectly balanced by the zesty flavors of garlic, Dijon, and anchovy paste. Garnished with shaved Parmigiano-Reggiano cheese and Romano-crusted croutons, this is a most savory experience.

6 (3/4-inch thick) slices French bread
grated Romano cheese
extra-virgin olive oil for drizzling
2 large hearts romaine, broken into bite-size pieces
2/3 cup shaved Parmigiano-Reggiano cheese (Use a vegetable peeler.)

Caesar Dressing:
salt and freshly ground pepper to taste
1 large clove garlic, crushed
1 teaspoon Dijon mustard
1/2 teaspoon anchovy paste
2 tablespoons mayonnaise
1 tablespoon lemon juice
1 tablespoon white wine vinegar
1/4 cup olive oil (not extra-virgin)

1. Make the croutons. Preheat the oven to 400°. Cut each slice of bread into quarters. Place on a baking sheet. Sprinkle with the Romano cheese and drizzle with the olive oil. Bake for 8 to 10 minutes until golden. (This may be done 6 to 8 hours in advance.)

2. Heap the romaine in a large bowl.

3. In a small bowl, whisk together the salt, pepper, garlic, Dijon, anchovy paste, mayonnaise, lemon juice, vinegar, and oil until thick and creamy.

4. Pour the dressing over the romaine and toss well until evenly coated. Garnish with the Parmesan and croutons and serve.

4 to 6 portions

THE CAPE CODDER

NOTATIONS

This is the ultimate harvest salad! Colorful and savory, it showcases the winning combination of apples, cranberries, glazed walnuts, and blue cheese. All is topped with a sweet, mouth-watering cranberry vinaigrette. To sample this dish is to love it.

14 cups bite-size pieces mixed greens (green leaf, red leaf, and Boston lettuces)
1 large Granny Smith apple, cored and cut into 3/4-inch cubes
1/2 cup dried cranberries
1/2 cup crumbled blue cheese
2/3 cup Glazed Walnuts (recipe follows)

Cranberry Vinaigrette:
salt and freshly ground pepper to taste
2 tablespoons diced shallot
1/4 cup whole berry cranberry sauce (homemade is preferable)
2 tablespoons cranberry juice
1 tablespoon red wine vinegar
1 tablespoon balsamic vinegar
1/3 cup olive oil (not extra-virgin)

1. Heap the greens in a large bowl. Add the apple, cranberries, and blue cheese.

2. In a separate small bowl, whisk together the salt, pepper, shallot, cranberry sauce, juice, vinegars, and oil until thick.

3. Pour the vinaigrette over the salad and toss well until evenly coated. Sprinkle with the glazed walnuts and serve.

4 to 6 portions

Glazed Walnuts:
1 tablespoon olive oil (not extra-virgin)
3 tablespoons sugar
2/3 cup coarsely chopped walnuts

Heat the oil in a small non-stick saucepan. Add the sugar and nuts, stirring until the sugar turns a caramel color. Working quickly so nuts don't burn, transfer the nuts and any glaze to a piece of parchment paper. Let cool for 30 minutes, then break into pieces. (This may be made 5 days in advance and stored in an air-tight tin.)

NOTATIONS

BURTON'S HARVEST SALAD

This salad features all the components we associate with the Thanksgiving feast. The lusty flavors of smoky bacon, sweet corn, tart cranberries, and toasted pecans bask in this salad that's lavished with a zesty, red wine vinaigrette.

1 large head or 2 hearts romaine, cut into 1-inch wide strips
1/4 pound bacon, cooked and coarsely chopped
1 cup cooked corn kernels
1/3 cup dried cranberries
1/2 cup chopped pecans, toasted
1/4 cup diced red onion

Red Wine Vinaigrette:
salt and freshly ground pepper to taste
1 large clove garlic, smashed
1 teaspoon Dijon mustard
dash of Worcestershire sauce
2 tablespoons red wine vinegar
1/2 cup extra-virgin olive oil

1. Heap the lettuce in a large bowl. Add the bacon, corn, cranberries, pecans, and onion.

2. In a separate small bowl, whisk together the salt, pepper, garlic, Dijon, Worcestershire sauce, vinegar, and oil until thick.

3. When ready to serve, remove the garlic from the dressing. Pour the vinaigrette over the salad, toss well, and present.

4 to 6 portions

MIXED GREENS WITH BALSAMIC GLAZE

NOTATIONS

Bacon-wrapped date nuggets (from my ***All-Occasion Cookbook***) are nestled in this colorful, mixed green salad that's finished with a balsamic glaze. This is on the far side of awesome!

5 ounces baby arugula
1 medium-size head radicchio, cut into 1/4-inch wide strips
2 endive, thinly sliced
12 Dates Marais (recipe follows)

Balsamic Glaze:
1/2 cup balsamic vinegar
salt and freshly ground pepper to taste
4 1/2 tablespoons extra-virgin olive oil

1. Heap the greens in a large bowl.

2. Make the balsamic glaze. Heat the balsamic vinegar in a small saucepan. Boil gently until syrupy and is reduced by half to 1/4 cup. Keep a watchful eye, as it can burn very easily. Let cool.

3. In a small bowl, whisk together the salt, pepper, 3 tablespoons reduced balsamic vinegar, and oil. (Reserve the extra balsamic for another use.)

4. Drizzle the dressing over the greens and toss gently until evenly coated. Divide the salad amongst individual plates and adorn each portion with 2 dates Marais. (Remove the toothpicks before serving.)

6 portions
Note—the extra reduced balsamic is wonderful drizzled over fresh strawberries or sliced navel oranges.

Dates Marais:
12 pitted dates
4 slices bacon, each slice cut into thirds

1. Preheat the oven to 375°.

2. Wrap each date in a piece of bacon and secure with a toothpick. (This may be prepared 2 days in advance and refrigerated, or made 3 weeks in advance and frozen. Thaw before proceeding.)

3. Bake for 10 minutes. Turn the dates over and bake for 5 to 10 minutes more until golden. Drain on a paper towel and serve.

GARDEN SALAD

NOTATIONS

A host of garden fresh vegetables sparkles in this presentation that sports a creamy mustard-tarragon vinaigrette. This makes a delightful main-dish salad when crowned with grilled chicken or shrimp.

1 large or 2 small heads Boston lettuce, torn into bite-size pieces
1/2 English cucumber, cut into 1/2-inch chunks
1 large carrot, coarsely grated
1/2 pound pencil-thin asparagus, cut into 1-inch lengths (If the asparagus spears are mature, peel the stalks.)
6 large or 8 small radishes, thinly sliced
1/2 cup chopped scallions

Mustard-Tarragon Vinaigrette:
salt and freshly ground pepper to taste
1 large clove garlic, smashed
1 tablespoon Dijon mustard
1 teaspoon dried tarragon
2 tablespoons tarragon vinegar
1/3 cup extra-virgin olive oil

1. Heap the lettuce in a large bowl. Add the cucumber, carrot, asparagus, radishes, and scallions.

2. In a separate small bowl, whisk together the salt, pepper, garlic, Dijon, tarragon, vinegar, and oil.

3. When ready to serve, remove the garlic from the dressing. Pour the vinaigrette over the salad, toss well, and serve at once.

4 to 6 portions

NOT YOUR AVERAGE JOE GREEN GODDESS

NOTATIONS

Originally created in the 1920s in San Francisco, this retro salad deserves a revival. The bright flavors of tarragon vinegar, chives, and anchovies make the mayonnaise-based dressing a classic.

1 head romaine, cut into bite-size pieces
14-ounce can artichoke hearts, rinsed, drained, and cut into quarters

Green Goddess Dressing:
salt and freshly ground pepper to taste
1/2 cup mayonnaise
1 clove garlic, crushed
1/2 teaspoon anchovy paste
1 teaspoon dried tarragon
1 tablespoon chopped chives
2 tablespoons chopped Italian parsley
1 tablespoon tarragon vinegar
1/2 tablespoon lemon juice

1. Heap the romaine in a large bowl. Add the artichoke hearts.

2. In a separate small bowl, whisk together the salt, pepper, mayonnaise, garlic, anchovy paste, and herbs. Add the vinegar and lemon juice and mix until smooth.

3. Pour the dressing over the salad, toss until evenly coated, and serve.

6 portions

CHAROSET SALAD

NOTATIONS

Modeled after the traditional Passover relish, this version of chopped apples and walnuts pairs well with pork and roast chicken. It also stands most gloriously alone. I leave the peel on the apples—it's more nutritious as well as more colorful!

1 large Granny Smith apple, cored and diced into 1/2-inch pieces
1 large Fuji apple, cored and diced into 1/2-inch pieces
3/4 cup chopped walnuts, toasted
2/3 cup pitted, chopped dates
1/2 cup raisins

Dressing:
1/4 cup sugar
3/4 to 1 teaspoon cinnamon
1/2 teaspoon ground ginger
salt to taste
1/4 cup Madeira or Ruby Port wine

1. Put the apples, walnuts, dates, and raisins in a large bowl. Stir until evenly mixed.

2. Put the sugar in a separate small bowl. Add the cinnamon, ginger, and salt and mix well. Add the wine and stir until evenly combined.

3. Pour the dressing over the apple mixture, toss well, and let marinate at room temperature for at least 2 hours and preferably for 3 or 4 hours. Serve at room temperature.

4 to 6 portions

SPRINGTIME CAPRESE SALAD

This beautiful and colorful presentation is a spin on the classic Caprese. Rounds of mozzarella are stacked with orange slices, decorated with fresh cherries, and drizzled with a sweet orange vinaigrette that's wonderful and refreshing.

1 pound buffalo mozzarella, sliced into 1/2-inch thick rounds
4 navel oranges, peeled and sliced into 1/2-inch thick rounds
15 cherries, pitted and halved (If fresh are unavailable, use canned, drained cherries.)

Orange Vinaigrette:
salt and freshly ground pepper to taste
1 1/2 tablespoons orange marmalade
1 tablespoon orange juice
3 tablespoons extra-virgin olive oil

1. On a platter, alternate the cheese and orange rounds. Sprinkle with the cherries.

2. In a small bowl, whisk together the salt, pepper, marmalade, orange juice, and oil until thick.

3. Drizzle the vinaigrette over the salad and serve.

6 to 8 portions

NOTATIONS

NOTATIONS

BOSTON LETTUCE WITH HONEY-MUSTARD VINAIGRETTE

This honey-mustard vinaigrette has become our house dressing. Light and delicately balanced, with the right amount of verve, it's sure to become your go-to preference. I always have some on hand in the refrigerator.

1 large or 2 small heads Boston lettuce, broken into bite-size pieces
1/2 pound mushrooms, sliced
1/2 English cucumber, halved lengthwise and sliced into 1/4-inch thick pieces
1 large carrot, coarsely grated

Honey-Mustard Vinaigrette:
salt and freshly ground pepper to taste
1 clove garlic, smashed
1 1/2 tablespoons Dijon mustard
1 tablespoon honey
2 tablespoons white wine vinegar
1/3 cup olive oil (not extra-virgin)

1. Heap the lettuce in a large bowl. Add the mushrooms, cucumber, and carrot.

2. In a separate small bowl, whisk together the salt, pepper, garlic, Dijon, honey, vinegar, and oil until thick and creamy.

3. When ready to serve, remove the garlic from the dressing. Pour the vinaigrette over the salad, toss well, and present.

4 to 6 portions

COLESLAW HENRI

NOTATIONS

Slaws make a colorful and festive addition to picnics and barbecues. This gustatory rendition stars a red cabbage base that's topped with celery, apple, and red grapes and napped in a honey-mustard mayonnaise.

1 small or 1/2 medium-size red cabbage, thinly sliced
2 large stalks celery, thinly sliced
1 large Granny Smith apple, cut into matchstick pieces
1 1/4 cups halved red seedless grapes

Honey-Mustard Mayonnaise:
salt and freshly ground pepper to taste
3 tablespoons Dijon mustard
1/4 cup honey
3/4 cup mayonnaise
1/4 cup cider vinegar

1. Heap the cabbage in a large bowl. Add the celery, apple, and grapes.

2. In a separate small bowl, whisk together the salt, pepper, Dijon, honey, and mayonnaise. Add the vinegar and stir until evenly combined.

3. Pour the dressing over the slaw mixture and toss well until evenly coated. Let marinate at room temperature for 30 minutes, stirring occasionally. Taste the slaw and adjust the seasoning if necessary and serve.

6 to 8 portions

DILLED-CABBAGE SLAW

NOTATIONS

The clean, crisp taste of fennel lends a nuance of flavor to this cabbage-based slaw. Complemented by a dill-mustard vinaigrette, it puts a new spin on an old-fashioned favorite.

1 small head cabbage, shredded
1 fennel bulb (fronds removed), thinly sliced
2 large stalks celery, thinly sliced
8 large radishes, thinly sliced

Dill-Mustard Vinaigrette:
1 teaspoon salt or more to taste
lots of freshly ground pepper
2 tablespoons Dijon mustard
1 tablespoon sugar
3 tablespoons chopped dill
3 tablespoons white wine vinegar
1/2 cup olive oil (not extra-virgin)

1. Heap the cabbage in a large bowl. Add the fennel, celery, and radishes.

2. In a separate small bowl, whisk together the salt, pepper, Dijon, sugar, dill, vinegar, and oil until thick and creamy.

3. Pour the dressing over the cabbage and mix well until evenly coated. Let marinate at room temperature for 1 to 2 hours. Taste the salad and adjust the seasoning if necessary—it may need more salt. Serve at room temperature.

8 portions

MEXICAN-STYLE CAESAR

NOTATIONS

Caesar takes on a different personality in this South-of-the-Border-inspired version. Embellished with ingredients indigenous to Mexican cuisine—corn, roasted red peppers, lime, and cornbread—this salad will titillate your taste buds.

1 (4-inch x 6-inch) piece cornbread, cut into 3/4-inch cubes
2 hearts romaine, cut into bite-size pieces
1 large roasted red pepper, cut into 1-inch pieces
1/2 cup cooked corn kernels
1/3 cup grated Manchego cheese (Spanish cheese)

Dressing:
salt and freshly ground pepper to taste
1 clove garlic, smashed
1 teaspoon Dijon mustard
1/4 cup mayonnaise
2 tablespoons lime juice
2 tablespoons extra-virgin olive oil

1. Make the cornbread croutons. Preheat the oven to 400°. Spread the cornbread chunks out in a single layer on a baking sheet. Bake for 10 minutes until golden.

2. Heap the romaine in a large bowl. Add the roasted pepper, corn, and cheese.

3. In a separate small bowl, whisk together the salt, pepper, garlic, Dijon, mayonnaise, lime juice, and oil until smooth and creamy.

4. When ready to serve, remove the garlic from the dressing. Pour the dressing over the salad and toss well. Garnish with the cornbread croutons and serve.

4 to 6 portions

THE DAILY SPECIAL

NOTATIONS

I love the crisp, fresh, anise-like flavor of fennel. It adds dimension to this simple green salad that's punctuated with craisins and finished with a lemony Parmesan vinaigrette. The fennel and Parmesan have a special affinity, making this the salad du jour.

12 to 14 cups bite-size pieces Boston lettuce
1 fennel bulb (fronds removed), thinly sliced
1/2 cup thinly sliced red onion
1/3 cup craisins

Parmesan Vinaigrette:
salt and freshly ground pepper to taste
1 teaspoon whole grain Dijon mustard
3 tablespoons finely grated Parmigiano-Reggiano cheese
2 tablespoons lemon juice
1/3 cup extra-virgin olive oil

1. Heap the lettuce in a large bowl. Add the fennel, onion, and craisins.

2. In a separate small bowl, whisk together the salt, pepper, Dijon, cheese, lemon juice, and oil until thick and creamy.

3. Pour the vinaigrette over the salad, toss well until evenly mixed, and serve at once.

4 to 6 portions

SALAD MUFFY

NOTATIONS

The mere mention of this composition sets my taste buds dancing! This mouth-watering salad is modeled after muffaletta, the famous New Orleans hero sandwich. Cloaked in an olive relish, this chopped salad spells delicious. The olive relish is also divine over grilled steak, burgers, chicken, or fish.

Olive Relish:
16 grape tomatoes, halved
1/2 cup pitted Kalamata olives, chopped
3/4 cup chopped small Manzanilla olives (pimiento-stuffed green olives)
1 large roasted red pepper, chopped
2 tablespoons capers
salt and freshly ground pepper to taste
1 clove garlic, smashed
1 teaspoon dried oregano
1/2 teaspoon dried thyme
2 tablespoons chopped Italian parsley
1/3 cup extra-virgin olive oil

1 head green leaf lettuce, chopped

1. Make the olive relish. In a medium-size bowl, heap the tomatoes. Add the olives, roasted pepper, and capers. Season with salt and pepper. Add the garlic, oregano, thyme, parsley, and oil, mixing well until evenly combined. Let marinate at room temperature for 2 to 3 hours.

2. Heap the lettuce in a large bowl.

3. When ready to serve, remove the garlic from the dressing. Pour the relish over the lettuce, toss well, and serve.

6 portions

MUSHROOM AND ENDIVE SALAD

NOTATIONS

Dijon and tarragon are the key ingredients that add pizzazz and personality to the mild-mannered fungus and endive combination, giving it zestful flavor.

4 endives, cut across the spears into 1/2-inch wide pieces
12 ounces white mushrooms, trimmed and sliced

Tarragon-Mustard Vinaigrette:
salt and freshly ground pepper to taste
2 tablespoons Dijon mustard
1 teaspoon dried tarragon
3 tablespoons tarragon vinegar
1/2 cup extra-virgin olive oil

1. Heap the endives and mushrooms in a large bowl.

2. In a separate small bowl, whisk together the salt, pepper, Dijon, tarragon, vinegar, and oil until thick and creamy.

3. Pour the vinaigrette over the salad, toss well, and serve at once.

4 to 6 portions

ORANGE, AVOCADO, AND HEARTS OF PALM SALAD

NOTATIONS

This lush salad couples sweet mandarin oranges with buttery avocado and delicate-flavored hearts of palm. Napped in a cilantro-lime vinaigrette, this South-of-the-Border composition will bring kudos to the chef.

1 large or 2 small heads Boston lettuce, broken into bite-size pieces
11-ounce can mandarin oranges, drained
14-ounce can hearts of palm, rinsed, drained, and cut into 1/2-inch thick rounds
1 Haas avocado, pitted, peeled, and cut into 3/4-inch chunks

Cilantro-Lime Vinaigrette:
salt and freshly ground pepper to taste
1 clove garlic, smashed
1 1/2 tablespoons orange marmalade
2 tablespoons finely chopped cilantro
2 tablespoons lime juice
1/3 cup extra-virgin olive oil

1. Heap the lettuce in a large bowl. Add the oranges, hearts of palm, and avocado.

2. In a separate small bowl, whisk together the salt, pepper, garlic, orange marmalade, cilantro, lime juice, and oil until thick.

3. When ready to serve, remove the garlic from the dressing. Pour the vinaigrette over the salad, toss gently, and present at once.

4 to 6 portions

NOTATIONS

PANZANELLA CAPRESE

This composition marries two of the great Italian classics—Panzanella, the rustic, chunky bread salad, with Caprese, the tomato and buffalo mozzarella medley. Dressed in a lusty pesto vinaigrette, the results are heavenly.

1/2 pound French bread, cut into 3/4-inch cubes, lightly toasted
4 medium-size tomatoes, coarsely chopped
3/4 pound buffalo mozzarella, cut into 3/4-inch cubes

Pesto Vinaigrette:
salt and freshly ground pepper to taste
1/2 cup pesto (see recipe, page 10)
2 tablespoons white wine vinegar
6 tablespoons extra-virgin olive oil

1. Heap the bread in a large bowl. Add the tomatoes and mozzarella.

2. In a separate small bowl, whisk together the salt, pepper, pesto, vinegar, and oil until smooth.

3. Pour the vinaigrette over the bread mixture, toss well until evenly coated, and serve at once.

6 portions

PAINT THE TOWN RED

NOTATIONS

A colorful array of all red-hued fruits and vegetables abounds in this composition that's cloaked in a cranberry vinaigrette. It's a feast for the eyes as well as the palate.

1 head red leaf lettuce, broken into bite-size pieces
1 medium-size head radicchio, broken into bite-size pieces
1 cup halved red seedless grapes
1 small red onion, thinly sliced
1/2 cup dried cranberries
1/3 cup pomegranate seeds

Cranberry Vinaigrette:
salt and freshly ground pepper to taste
1 clove garlic, smashed
1/4 cup cranberry sauce, melted
2 tablespoons red wine vinegar
1/3 cup extra-virgin olive oil

1. Heap the lettuce and radicchio in a large bowl. Add the grapes, onion, cranberries, and pomegranate seeds.

2. In a separate small bowl, whisk together the salt, pepper, garlic, cranberry sauce, vinegar, and olive oil until thick. Let marinate for 15 to 20 minutes.

3. When ready to serve, remove the garlic from the dressing. Pour the vinaigrette over the salad, toss well, and serve.

6 to 8 portions

PEACHES AND TOMATOES

NOTATIONS

Juicy, sweet, and delicious are apt words to describe this stylish salad. Chopped peaches and tomatoes strut a yummy, white balsamic vinaigrette for a fresh taste of summer. White balsamic vinegar is made from white wine vinegar and sweet Trebbiano grape must. It's mild, delicate flavor lends a special touch to the vinaigrette.

10 ounces mesclun
2 medium-size peaches, pitted, and cut into 3/4-inch chunks
18 cherry or grape tomatoes, halved

White Balsamic Vinaigrette:
salt and freshly ground pepper to taste
1 medium-size shallot, diced
1 tablespoon honey
2 tablespoons white balsamic vinegar
1/3 cup extra-virgin olive oil

1. Heap the mesclun in a large bowl. Add the peaches and tomatoes.

2. In a separate small bowl, whisk together the salt, pepper, shallot, honey, vinegar, and oil.

3. Pour the vinaigrette over the salad, toss well, and serve at once.

6 portions

PEACH CAPRESE SALAD

NOTATIONS

Peaches share center stage with buffalo mozzarella and mixed berries in this vibrant summer salad. Garnished with a basil chiffonade and drizzled with a balsamic glaze, it's a feast for the eyes as well as the palate. Serve it as a salad, an appetizer, or even dessert!

1 cup balsamic vinegar
6 ripe peaches (or nectarines), sliced in half and pitted
1 pound buffalo mozzarella, cut into 1/3-inch thick rounds
1/2 cup blueberries
1/2 cup raspberries
12 large basil leaves, julienned (chiffonade)
salt to taste

1. Reduce the balsamic vinegar. Put the vinegar in a small saucepan and bring to a boil over medium heat. Reduce the heat to low and simmer gently until vinegar is syrupy and reduced to 1/3 cup, about 8 to 9 minutes. (Keep a close watch, as it can burn very easily.) Let cool.

2. Slice each peach half into 4 wedges; slice each cheese round into 6 wedges.

3. On each of 6 plates, arrange an equal number of peach wedges. Alternate the fruit with wedges of cheese. Sprinkle with the blueberries and raspberries, and garnish with the basil chiffonade.

4. Season with salt. Drizzle each serving with 1/2 to 1 tablespoon reduced balsamic vinegar and serve.

6 portions

NOTATIONS

FRENCH-STYLE POTATO SALAD

I have taken the classic potato salad and given it a French twist. Yukon Golds are the potatoes of choice. Their creamy texture best absorbs the luscious tarragon-Dijon vinaigrette that's spruced up with capers and cornichons. This makes great picnic fare.

1 1/2 pounds Yukon Gold potatoes, cut into 1-inch chunks
2/3 cup chopped celery
1/2 cup thinly sliced scallions

Tarragon-Dijon Vinaigrette:
salt and freshly ground pepper to taste
1 tablespoon Dijon mustard
1 tablespoon capers
1 tablespoon chopped cornichons
1 teaspoon dried tarragon
2 tablespoons finely chopped curly parsley
2 tablespoons tarragon vinegar
1/3 cup extra-virgin olive oil

1. Boil the potatoes in salted water until fork tender, about 10 minutes. Drain well and transfer to a large bowl.

2. While the potatoes are cooking, prepare the vinaigrette. In a small bowl, whisk together the salt, pepper, Dijon, capers, cornichons, tarragon, parsley, vinegar, and oil until thick and creamy.

3. Add the celery and scallions to the potatoes.

4. While the potatoes are still hot, pour the vinaigrette over the salad and toss well until evenly coated. The potatoes will absorb more flavor when they are warm. Serve warm or at room temperature.

6 portions

WARM GERMAN-STYLE POTATO SALAD

NOTATIONS

This classic German potato salad stands on its laurels. Red-skinned potatoes, bacon, onion, and a bacon-flavored, mustard vinaigrette distinguish this most seductive salad. Serve it alongside grilled sausages, chicken, or burgers.

4 slices thick-cut bacon
1½ pounds red-skinned potatoes, cut into 1-inch chunks
½ cup diced red onion
2 tablespoons chopped Italian parsley

Mustard Vinaigrette:
salt and freshly ground pepper to taste
1 teaspoon sugar
1 tablespoon whole grain Dijon mustard
2 tablespoons cider vinegar
3 tablespoons olive oil (not extra-virgin)
2 tablespoons reserved bacon fat

1. Cook the bacon in a skillet until golden and crisp. Remove the bacon from the pan. Reserve 2 tablespoons of the bacon fat.

2. Coarsely chop the bacon.

3. Prepare the vinaigrette. In a small bowl, whisk together the salt, pepper, sugar, Dijon, vinegar, oil, and bacon fat.

4. Boil the potatoes in salted water until fork tender, about 10 minutes. Drain well and transfer to a large bowl. Add the bacon, onion, and parsley.

5. Pour the vinaigrette over the warm potatoes, toss well, and serve at once.

6 portions

SALAD MARCHÉ

NOTATIONS

Delicate leaves of mesclun are coarsely chopped, generously sprinkled with toasted hazelnuts, and lightly coated with a hazelnut vinaigrette. I simply love the rich, nutty taste the hazelnuts impart to this composition.

10 ounces mesclun, coarsely chopped
2/3 cup chopped hazelnuts, toasted, skins rubbed off

Hazelnut Vinaigrette:
salt to taste
1 1/4 teaspoons sugar
1 tablespoon red wine vinegar
1 1/2 tablespoons hazelnut oil
2 1/2 tablespoons olive oil (not extra-virgin)

1. Heap the mesclun in a large bowl. Add the hazelnuts.

2. In a separate small bowl, whisk together the salt, sugar, vinegar, and oils.

3. Pour the vinaigrette over the salad, toss well until evenly coated, and serve at once.

4 to 6 portions

REDS AND GREENS

This colorful mélange of contrasts—red and green leaf lettuces—struts a luscious, creamy, mustard dressing. Garnished with sieved hard-boiled egg, this dish is mouth-wateringly delicious.

NOTATIONS

1 small head red leaf lettuce, broken into bite-size pieces
1 head Boston lettuce, broken into bite-size pieces
2 hard-boiled eggs, sieved

Creamy Mustard Vinaigrette:
salt and freshly ground pepper to taste
2 tablespoons whole grain Dijon mustard
2 teaspoons capers
1/4 cup heavy cream
1 1/2 tablespoons sherry vinegar
2 tablespoons olive oil (not extra-virgin)

1. Heap the lettuces in a large bowl. Add the eggs.

2. In a separate small bowl, whisk together the salt, pepper, Dijon, capers, cream, vinegar, and oil until thick and creamy.

3. Pour the vinaigrette over the salad, toss well until evenly mixed, and serve at once.

4 to 6 portions

SALAD MASSIMO

NOTATIONS

Rather than overpower baby romaine with croutons, I've chosen to use toasted, coarse French bread crumbs instead as a garnish for this salad. The crunchy nuggets enhance the delicate, tender leaves, and all is dressed in a mouth-watering, white balsamic vinaigrette.

1 cup coarse French bread crumbs
4 teaspoons extra-virgin olive oil
salt to taste
10 ounces baby romaine

White Balsamic Vinaigrette:
salt and freshly ground pepper to taste
1 teaspoon Dijon mustard
1 medium-size shallot, diced
2 tablespoons white balsamic vinegar
1/3 cup extra-virgin olive oil

1. Preheat the oven to 400°.

2. Place the bread crumbs in a bowl. Drizzle with the olive oil and season with salt. Toss well until evenly coated. Place the crumbs in an even layer on a baking sheet. Bake for 6 to 8 minutes until golden.

3. Heap the baby romaine in a large bowl. Garnish with the toasted bread crumbs.

4. In a separate small bowl, whisk together the salt, pepper, Dijon, shallot, vinegar, and oil until thick and creamy.

5. Pour the vinaigrette over the salad, toss well, and serve at once.

4 to 6 portions

SALAD ROMESCO

NOTATIONS

Spanish in design and delicious in taste, this salad sports a romaine base crowned with toasted pita chips and Romesco sauce. Romesco is a classic Spanish sauce that's typified by a thick purée of roasted peppers, garlic, almonds, and olive oil. I've altered it slightly for this dish, leaving it chunky. It transforms the ordinary green salad into an extraordinary eating experience!

Romesco Sauce:
1 large roasted red pepper, chopped
1/3 cup slivered almonds, toasted and chopped
salt and freshly ground pepper to taste
1 large clove garlic, minced
generous 1/4 teaspoon smoked paprika
2 tablespoons chopped Italian parsley
1 1/2 tablespoons extra-virgin olive oil

1 head or 2 hearts romaine, cut into 3/4-inch wide strips
1 medium-size pita bread (7-inch round), toasted until crisp and broken into bite-size pieces

Vinaigrette:
salt and freshly ground pepper to taste
1 teaspoon Dijon mustard
1 1/2 tablespoons red wine vinegar
1/2 tablespoon sherry vinegar
1/3 cup extra-virgin olive oil

1. Make the Romesco Sauce. In a medium-size bowl, combine the roasted pepper, almonds, salt, pepper, garlic, paprika, parsley, and oil. Let marinate for 1 to 2 hours at room temperature, and as much as 24 hours refrigerated. (Return to room temperature before using.)

2. Heap the lettuce in a large bowl.

3. In a separate small bowl, whisk together the salt, pepper, Dijon, vinegars, and oil until thick and creamy.

4. Add the Romesco sauce to the lettuce. Pour the vinaigrette over the salad and toss well. Garnish with the toasted pita chips and serve at once.

6 portions

SHEPARD'S SALAD

NOTATIONS

This is your typical Middle Eastern salad. It stars a host of garden-fresh, chopped vegetables in a light vinaigrette, making this a refreshing and colorful summertime dish. I love to pair this with grilled lamb or chicken skewers and pita bread.

3 medium-size tomatoes, seeded, diced into 1/2-inch pieces, and drained
1 cucumber, peeled and diced into 1/2-inch pieces
1 green pepper, diced into 1/2-inch pieces
3 scallions, sliced into 1/2-inch rounds
1/2 medium-size red onion, diced
1/2 cup coarsely chopped Italian parsley

Vinaigrette:
at least 1 teaspoon salt (preferably sea salt)
freshly ground pepper to taste
2 tablespoons lemon juice
2 tablespoons red wine vinegar
1/4 cup extra-virgin olive oil

1. Put the tomatoes, cucumber, pepper, scallions, onion, and parsley a large bowl.

2. In a separate small bowl, whisk together the salt, pepper, lemon juice, vinegar, and oil.

3. Pour the dressing over the chopped vegetables, toss well, and let marinate at room temperature for at least 30 minutes. Taste the salad and adjust the seasoning if necessary—you may need to add more salt. Serve at room temperature.

4 to 6 portions

SONOMA SALAD

NOTATIONS

Fennel is the hallmark ingredient in this composition. The anise-flavored bulb is known for its clean, crisp taste and crunchy texture. It pairs well with cucumber, dill, and goat cheese in this lush salad.

2 medium-size heads Boston lettuce, separated into individual leaves
1/2 fennel bulb (fronds removed), very thinly sliced
1 large or 2 small pickling cucumbers, peeled and thinly sliced
1/4 cup thinly sliced scallions
4 ounces chèvre, crumbled

Dill-Cream Dressing:
salt and freshly ground pepper to taste
1 tablespoon chopped dill
1/4 cup crème fraîche
2 tablespoons white wine vinegar
1/3 cup olive oil (not extra-virgin)

1. Heap the lettuce in a large bowl. Add the fennel, cucumber, scallions, and chèvre.

2. In a separate small bowl, whisk together the salt, pepper, dill, crème fraîche, vinegar, and oil until thick and creamy.

3. Pour the dressing over the salad, toss well, and serve at once.

4 to 6 portions

SIMPLY SPINACH

NOTATIONS

Spinach is one of the dark, leafy greens rich in vitamins and iron. Prized for its clean, delicate, flavor, it's served with a simple, lemon-Parmesan vinaigrette to be enjoyed by all.

7 ounces baby spinach

Lemon Vinaigrette:
salt and freshly ground pepper to taste
2 tablespoons lemon juice
$4^1/_2$ tablespoons extra-virgin olive oil
$1^1/_2$ tablespoons finely grated Parmigiano-Reggiano cheese

1. Heap the spinach in a large bowl.

2. In a separate small bowl, whisk together the salt, pepper, lemon juice, oil, and Parmesan until thick and creamy.

3. Pour the vinaigrette over the spinach, toss well, and serve at once.

4 portions

SPINACH, ORANGE, AND CRANBERRY SALAD

NOTATIONS

The contrasting colors, tastes, and textures of this dish are dynamic. Leaves of baby spinach form the base for succulent mandarin oranges, tart, dried cranberries, and crunchy Marcona almonds. All is complemented by a mouth-watering, orange-balsamic vinaigrette.

10 ounces baby spinach
2 (11-ounce) cans mandarin oranges, drained
1/3 cup dried cranberries
1/3 cup Marcona almonds, coarsely chopped

Orange-Balsamic Vinaigrette:
salt and freshly ground pepper to taste
1 clove garlic, smashed
1 teaspoon Dijon mustard
1 1/2 tablespoons orange marmalade
2 tablespoons balsamic vinegar
1/3 cup extra-virgin olive oil

1. Heap the spinach in a large bowl. Add the oranges, cranberries, and almonds.

2. In a separate small bowl, whisk together the salt, pepper, garlic, Dijon, orange marmalade, vinegar, and oil until thick and creamy.

3. When ready to serve, remove the garlic from the dressing. Pour the vinaigrette over the salad, toss gently until evenly mixed, and serve at once.

6 portions

SPINACH AND STRAWBERRIES

NOTATIONS

Strawberries are a member of the rose family; therefore, they should have a lush, fragrant bouquet. Let your nose be your guide when purchasing these juicy berries. The juxtaposition of the red fruit set against the dark green spinach in this dish makes it colorful and vibrant. Dressed in a strawberry-balsamic vinaigrette, it's a definite crowd pleaser.

10 ounces baby spinach
1 quart strawberries, hulled and thickly sliced
1/3 cup shelled pistachio nuts

Strawberry-Balsamic Vinaigrette:
salt and freshly ground pepper to taste
1 tablespoon diced shallot
2 tablespoons strawberry preserves
2 tablespoons balsamic vinegar
5 tablespoons extra-virgin olive oil

1. Heap the spinach in a large bowl. Add the strawberries and pistachios.

2. In a separate small bowl, whisk together the salt, pepper, shallot, strawberry preserves, vinegar, and oil until thick and creamy.

3. Pour the dressing over the salad, toss well, and serve at once.

6 portions

TAPAS SALAD

NOTATIONS

Ingredients indigenous to Spanish cuisine—spinach, roasted peppers, and almonds—are showcased in this salad that glistens with a sherry vinaigrette. I've chosen to use agave nectar to sweeten the dressing instead of honey. Agave is a liquid sweetener that's made from the succulent leaves of the agave plant.

10 ounces baby spinach
2 roasted red peppers, cut into 3/4-inch pieces
1/3 cup raisins, plumped in hot water for 2 minutes, drained
1/2 cup smoked almonds, coarsely chopped

Sherry Vinaigrette:
salt and freshly ground pepper to taste
1 clove garlic, smashed
1 tablespoon amber agave nectar
2 tablespoons sherry vinegar
1/3 cup extra-virgin olive oil

1. Heap the spinach in a large bowl. Add the roasted peppers, raisins, and almonds.

2. In a separate small bowl, whisk together the salt, pepper, garlic, agave, vinegar, and oil.

3. When ready to serve, remove the garlic from the dressing. Pour the vinaigrette over the salad, toss well, and serve.

6 portions

MIXED GREENS WITH OLIVE VINAIGRETTE

NOTATIONS

Of Greek origin, Kalamata olives are prized for their purple-black color and distinct, rich flavor. This mixed green salad sports a Kalamata olive vinaigrette that turns the ordinary into the extraordinary.

12 to 14 cups bite-size pieces romaine
1 1/2 cups bite-size pieces radicchio
1/4 cup very thinly sliced red onion

Olive Vinaigrette:
salt and freshly ground pepper to taste
1 clove garlic, smashed
1/4 cup chopped Kalamata olives
2 tablespoons juice from Kalamata olive jar
2 tablespoons red wine vinegar
2 tablespoons olive oil (not extra-virgin)
1/4 cup extra-virgin olive oil

1. Heap the lettuces in a large bowl. Garnish with the onion.

2. In a separate small bowl, whisk together the salt, pepper, garlic, chopped olives, olive juice, vinegar, and oils.

3. When ready to serve, remove the garlic from the dressing. Pour the vinaigrette over the salad, toss well, and serve.

6 portions

STOLI SALAD

NOTATIONS

A palette of classic Russian ingredients—potatoes, cucumber, tomatoes, onion, and dill—abounds in this most fashionable, yet simple salad. It's a definite crowd pleaser.

2 medium-size red-skinned potatoes, cut into 3/4-inch chunks
2 hearts romaine, chopped
2 medium-large tomatoes, each cut into 12 wedges
2 large pickling cucumbers (or 1 large garden cucumber), peeled, halved lengthwise, and thinly sliced
1/2 small red onion, thinly sliced

Dill Vinaigrette:
1/2 teaspoon salt
freshly ground pepper to taste
1 clove garlic, smashed
2 tablespoons chopped dill
2 tablespoons white wine vinegar
1/3 cup olive oil (not extra-virgin)

1. Boil the potatoes in salted water until fork tender, about 10 to 12 minutes. Drain well and let cool.

2. Heap the lettuce in a large bowl. Add the potatoes, tomatoes, cucumber, and onion.

3. In a separate small bowl, whisk together the salt, pepper, garlic, dill, vinegar, and oil.

4. When ready to serve, remove the garlic from the dressing. Pour the vinaigrette over the salad, toss well, and present.

4 to 6 portions

NOTATIONS

BOSTON LETTUCE WITH TOMATO-CORN RELISH

This salad celebrates the bounty of the summer season. Lush with garden tomatoes and sweet corn, accented with scallions and red pepper, and dressed in a sweet cider vinaigrette, this colorful mélange abounds with flavor. The relish is also fabulous over grilled chicken or fish.

Tomato-Corn Relish:
12 cherry tomatoes, halved
1 1/2 cups cooked corn kernels
1/2 cup diced red pepper
1/4 cup thinly sliced scallions
salt and freshly ground pepper to taste
2 tablespoons sugar
1/4 cup cider vinegar
2 tablespoons olive oil (not extra-virgin)

12 cups bite-size pieces Boston lettuce

1. In a medium-size bowl, combine the tomatoes, corn, red pepper, and scallions.

2. In a separate small bowl, whisk together the salt, pepper, sugar, vinegar, and oil.

3. Pour the dressing over the tomato-corn mixture and stir until evenly coated. Let marinate at room temperature for 1 to 2 hours.

4. When ready to serve, heap the lettuce in a large bowl. Pour the marinated relish over the greens, toss well, and present.

4 to 6 portions

LETTUCE, TOMATO, AND EGG SALAD

NOTATIONS

A bed of romaine provides the background for lush garden tomatoes and chopped hard-boiled eggs, which have a curious affinity. All is tossed in a zesty vinaigrette that's akin to Caesar dressing.

2 hearts romaine, cut into 3/4-inch wide strips
2 large tomatoes, coarsely chopped
4 hard-boiled eggs, coarsely chopped

Dressing:
salt and freshly ground pepper to taste
1 clove garlic, smashed
1 teaspoon Dijon mustard
generous 1/2 teaspoon anchovy paste
3 tablespoons finely grated Parmigiano-Reggiano cheese
2 tablespoons red wine vinegar
6 tablespoons extra-virgin olive oil

1. Heap the romaine in a large bowl. Add the tomatoes and eggs.

2. In a separate small bowl, whisk together the salt, pepper, garlic, Dijon, anchovy paste, cheese, vinegar, and oil until thick and creamy.

3. When ready to serve, remove the garlic from the dressing. Pour the vinaigrette over the salad, toss gently until evenly mixed, and serve.

4 to 6 portions

NOTATIONS

BAKED TOMATOES PROVENÇAL

Ripe garden tomatoes are sliced in half, encrusted with a lush pesto-flavored bread crumb topping, and then baked to a turn. It doesn't get better than this!

3 large, ripe tomatoes, cut in half across the middle horizontally
1/2 cup fresh bread crumbs
1/4 cup finely grated Parmigiano-Reggiano cheese
salt and freshly ground pepper to taste
1 clove garlic, crushed
1 teaspoon dried basil
3 tablespoons chopped Italian parsley
1/4 cup extra-virgin olive oil
Boston lettuce leaves

1. Preheat the oven to 350°. Set the tomatoes in a baking dish, cut side up.

2. In a bowl, combine the bread crumbs, Parmesan cheese, salt, pepper, garlic, basil, parsley, and oil. Mix well until evenly combined.

3. Place equal amounts of the bread crumb mixture atop each tomato, pressing down gently.

4. Bake for 20 minutes until cooked and browned. Serve hot, warm, or at room temperature atop Boston lettuce.

4 to 6 portions

SALAD BELUCCA

NOTATIONS

All you BLT lovers take heed! The infamous trio of ingredients is further enhanced by fruity avocado, making this the ultimate BLT experience. It offers layers of flavors--sweet, garden tomatoes, smoky bacon, rich, buttery avocado, and a Parmesan-walnut vinaigrette. This is sure to win rave reviews.

14 cups bite-size pieces Boston lettuce
2 medium-size tomatoes, cut into 1-inch chunks
6 slices bacon, cooked until crisp and coarsely chopped
1 ripe Haas avocado, pitted, peeled, and cut into 1-inch chunks

Parmesan-Walnut Vinaigrette:
salt and freshly ground pepper to taste
2 tablespoons finely grated Parmigiano-Reggiano cheese
1 1/2 tablespoons sherry vinegar
2 tablespoons walnut oil
1/4 cup extra-virgin olive oil

1. Heap the lettuce in a large bowl. Add the tomatoes, bacon, and avocado.

2. In a separate small bowl, whisk together the salt, pepper, cheese, vinegar, and oils until thick.

3. Pour the vinaigrette over the salad, toss gently until evenly dressed, and serve at once.

4 to 6 portions

SALAD TUSCANY

NOTATIONS

This composition basks in the glory of the Italian palette. Figs, prosciutto, Parmesan cheese, and pine nuts reflect the rich flavors of the Mediterranean, creating a most seductive salad. The balsamic-based vinaigrette is sweetened with agave nectar, creating the perfect balance of flavors.

1 head green leaf lettuce, broken into bite-size pieces
1/2 cup chopped, dried Calimyrna figs (each quartered)
1/8 pound thinly sliced prosciutto, cut into 1-inch by 3-inch strips
1/4 cup pine nuts, toasted
1/2 cup coarsely grated Parmigiano-Reggiano cheese

Balsamic Vinaigrette:
salt and freshly ground pepper to taste
1 clove garlic, smashed
1 tablespoon Dijon mustard
1 1/2 teaspoons amber agave nectar
2 tablespoons balsamic vinegar
6 tablespoons extra-virgin olive oil

1. Heap the lettuce in a large bowl. Add the figs, prosciutto, and pine nuts.

2. In a separate small bowl, whisk together the salt, pepper, garlic, Dijon, agave, vinegar, and oil until thick and creamy.

3. When ready to serve, remove the garlic from the dressing. Pour the vinaigrette over the salad and toss until evenly mixed. Garnish with the Parmesan and serve.

4 to 6 portions

VILLAGE SALAD

NOTATIONS

Tomatoes, artichoke hearts, and avocado form the perfect trio atop romaine. Finished with a creamy, lemon-basil dressing, this salad shines with savory, buttery flavors.

1 large head romaine, broken into bite-size pieces
12 cherry tomatoes, halved
14-ounce can artichoke hearts, rinsed, drained, and cut into quarters
1 Haas avocado, pitted, peeled, and coarsely chopped

Lemon-Basil Dressing:
salt and freshly ground pepper to taste
1 teaspoon Dijon mustard
1 teaspoon dried basil
1/4 cup mayonnaise
2 tablespoons lemon juice
2 tablespoons extra-virgin olive oil

1. Heap the romaine in a large bowl. Add the tomatoes, artichokes, and avocado.

2. In a separate small bowl, whisk together the salt, pepper, Dijon, basil, mayonnaise, lemon juice, and oil until thick and creamy.

3. Pour the dressing over the salad, toss gently until evenly mixed, and serve.

4 to 6 portions

NOTATIONS

WATERMELON AND CUCUMBER SALAD

This light and refreshing summertime salad is blushing with juicy watermelon, crunchy cucumber, and tangy feta, and is offset by a lemony, mint dressing.

4 cups seedless watermelon, cut into 1/2-inch cubes
2 cups seedless cucumber, cut into 1/2-inch cubes
1/4 pound feta cheese, cut into 1/2-inch cubes
1/2 cup sliced red onion

Mint Vinaigrette:
1/2 teaspoon sea salt
1/4 cup finely chopped mint
1 tablespoon lemon juice
2 tablespoons extra-virgin olive oil

1. Put the watermelon in a large glass bowl. Add the cucumber, feta, and onion.

2. In a separate small bowl, whisk together the salt, mint, lemon juice, and oil.

3. Pour the dressing over the salad, toss gently until evenly coated, and serve at once.

4 to 6 portions

ZUCCHINI RIBBON SLAW

NOTATIONS

The Middle Eastern flavor of feta, dill, lemon, and extra-virgin olive oil dominate this composition of thinly sliced "ribbons" of zucchini. Absolutely delicious and fun to eat, this simple salad is a prize winner.

3 medium-size zucchini
2/3 cup crumbled goat's or sheep's milk feta cheese

Lemon Vinaigrette:
salt and freshly ground pepper to taste
1 tablespoon chopped dill
2 tablespoons lemon juice
3 tablespoons extra-virgin olive oil

1. Using a mandolin, slice the zucchini lengthwise into thin ribbons, stopping shy of the seed core; then rotate the zucchini 1/4 turn and slice. Continue rotating and slicing until all sides have been sliced. Discard the seed core.

2. Put the zucchini in a medium-size bowl. Add the feta.

3. In a separate small bowl, whisk together the salt, pepper, dill, lemon juice, and oil.

4. Pour the vinaigrette over the zucchini, toss well, and serve.

4 portions

PASTA, BEAN AND GRAIN SALADS

NOTATIONS

PENNE, ASPARAGUS, AND SUN-DRIED TOMATO SALAD

Penne provides the background for this vibrant salad that pairs asparagus with rich-flavored sun-dried tomatoes. Dressed in a Dijon vinaigrette, it adds pizzazz to an already stellar dish.

12 ounces penne or ziti
1 1/4 pounds asparagus (if stalks are mature, peeled), cut into 2-inch lengths, and steamed until tender-crisp, about 3 minutes
2/3 cup sun-dried tomatoes, hydrated in hot water for 1 minute, drained, and coarsely chopped

Dijon Vinaigrette:
salt and freshly ground pepper to taste
1 1/2 tablespoons Dijon mustard
1 large clove garlic, crushed
2 tablespoons capers
2 tablespoons white wine vinegar
6 tablespoons extra-virgin olive oil

1. Cook the pasta according to the package directions. Drain well and transfer to a large bowl.

2. While the pasta is cooking, make the vinaigrette. In a small bowl, whisk together the salt, pepper, Dijon, garlic, capers, vinegar, and oil until thick and creamy.

3. Add the asparagus and sun-dried tomatoes to the freshly cooked pasta.

4. Pour the vinaigrette over the pasta, toss well, and serve warm or at room temperature.

6 to 8 portions

PASTA WITH EGGPLANT RELISH

NOTATIONS

Is it ratatouille or caponata? Actually, it's a cross between the two, capturing the best of both dishes. The Mediterranean relish is a bountiful mixture of garden vegetables, punctuated with olives and raisins, and complemented by a sweet-tart balsamic sauce. It also makes an outstanding topping for grilled chicken, veal, or burgers.

1/4 cup extra-virgin olive oil
1 medium-size yellow onion, diced into 1/2-inch pieces
1 large clove garlic, minced
1 medium-size zucchini, diced into 1/2-inch pieces
1 Italian eggplant (about 10 ounces), diced into 1/2-pieces
1 red pepper, diced into 1/2-inch pieces
salt and freshly ground pepper to taste
16-ounce can diced tomatoes
1/2 cup raisins
1/2 cup small Manzanilla olives (pimiento-stuffed green olives)
2 tablespoons tomato paste
1 teaspoon dried oregano
1/4 cup chopped Italian parsley
2 teaspoons sugar
2 tablespoons balsamic vinegar
1 pound fusilli

1. Heat the oil in a large non-stick fry pan. Add the onion and garlic and cook for 1 minute.

2. Add the zucchini, eggplant, and red pepper to the skillet. Season with salt and pepper. Cover and cook over medium-high heat for 10 to 12 minutes until the vegetables are softened, stirring occasionally.

3. Add the diced tomatoes, raisins, olives, tomato paste, oregano, parsley, sugar, and vinegar. Cover and let simmer for 15 to 20 minutes. (This may be made up to 2 days in advance and refrigerated. Reheat before serving.)

4. Cook the pasta according to the package directions. Drain well and transfer to a large bowl.

5. Add the relish to the freshly cooked pasta, toss well until evenly mixed, and serve hot, warm, or at room temperature.

6 to 8 portions

NOTATIONS

PENNE, GREEN BEAN, AND PANCETTA SALAD

Pancetta is Italian-style bacon that is cured, not smoked. It's cured with salt, pepper, and spices, lending a spicy-sweet quality to the flavor and has a more mellow taste than bacon. If you can't find pancetta, you can substitute bacon in the recipe.

12 ounces penne
4 to 5 ounces pancetta, cooked until golden and coarsely chopped
1/2 pound green beans, steamed until tender-crisp, about 5 minutes

Sherry Vinaigrette:
salt and freshly ground pepper to taste
1 tablespoon Dijon mustard
1 1/2 tablespoons sherry vinegar
6 tablespoons extra-virgin olive oil

1. Cook the pasta according to the package directions. Drain well and transfer to a large bowl.

2. While the pasta is cooking, make the vinaigrette. In a small bowl, whisk together the salt, pepper, Dijon, vinegar, and oil until thick and creamy.

3. Add the pancetta and green beans to the pasta.

4. Pour the vinaigrette over the warm pasta, toss well until evenly coated, and serve warm or at room temperature.

6 to 8 portions

PASTA WITH ROASTED SAUSAGES AND GRAPES

NOTATIONS

This could be my new go-to pasta salad. Not only is it quick and easy to make, it's also absolutely delicious. Roasted sausages and grapes are glazed in a savory balsamic-Port wine marinade, tossed with penne, and dusted with Parmigiano-Reggiano. The sweet grapes are a perfect counterpoint to the spicy sausages, balancing the flavors of the dish. This makes for a memorable feast.

1 pound chicken sausages (combination of sweet and hot)
1 1/2 cups seedless grapes (combination of red and green)
salt and freshly ground pepper to taste
2 tablespoons balsamic vinegar
1/4 cup Ruby Port wine
3 tablespoons extra-virgin olive oil
12 ounces penne
1/4 cup chopped Italian parsley
1/2 cup grated Parmigiano-Reggiano cheese

1. Put the sausages and grapes in a bowl.

2. In a separate small bowl, mix the salt, pepper, vinegar, wine, and oil.

3. Pour the marinade over the sausage mixture and toss well until evenly coated. Let marinate for 30 minutes, stirring occasionally.

4. Preheat the oven to 400°.

5. Transfer the sausage mixture to a non-stick 9 x 13-inch roasting pan in a single layer. Drizzle with all of the marinade.

6. Roast for 10 minutes. Turn the sausages over and roast for 10 minutes more. Remove from the oven and cut the sausages into 1/2-inch thick rounds.

7. While the sausages are roasting, cook the pasta according to the package directions. Drain well and transfer to a large bowl.

8. Add the roasted sausages, grapes, and any pan juices to the pasta. Toss well until evenly coated. Garnish with the parsley and cheese and serve hot, warm, or at room temperature.

6 or more portions

NOTATIONS

PASTA, TOMATO, AND CHICKPEA SALAD

This gusty pasta salad showcases an array of Mediterranean ingredients. Fusilli is replete with tomatoes, chickpeas, olives, and pine nuts. Dressed in a lemon-basil vinaigrette, it definitely has the wow factor.

3/4 pound fusilli, cooked according to package directions
1 1/2 cups halved cherry or grape tomatoes
1 1/4 cups canned chickpeas, rinsed and drained
1/2 cup sliced pimiento-stuffed green olives
1/4 cup pine nuts, toasted

Lemon-Basil Vinaigrette:
salt and freshly ground pepper to taste
1/4 cup chopped basil
1/2 cup chopped Italian parsley
2 1/2 tablespoons lemon juice
1/2 cup extra-virgin olive oil

1. Heap the pasta in a large bowl. Add the tomatoes, chickpeas, olives, and pine nuts.

2. In a separate small bowl, whisk together the salt, pepper, basil, parsley, lemon juice, and oil.

3. Pour the vinaigrette over the salad, toss well until evenly combined, and serve at room temperature.

6 or 8 portions

PASTA, TOMATO, AND CORN SALAD

NOTATIONS

Lush, juicy tomatoes and sweet, fresh corn are the ultimate summertime pairing. When combined with pasta and bathed in pesto, it's the best! This is a great dish for picnics, barbecues, and buffets. If you want, you can add grilled shrimp or chicken for a 5-star experience.

3 large ears corn, husked
olive oil (not extra-virgin)
salt
3/4 pound penne or fusilli
1 pint grape tomatoes, halved
1 1/4 cups pesto (see recipe, page 10)
4 ounces chèvre, crumbled

1. Preheat the oven to 450°. Place the ears of corn on a baking sheet. Rub with olive oil and season with salt. Roast for 12 minutes. Let cool and then remove the kernels from the cob. Put the corn in a large bowl.

2. Cook the pasta according to the package directions and drain well.

3. Add the pasta and tomatoes to the corn. Season with salt.

4. While the pasta is still warm, pour the pesto on top and mix well until evenly combined . Garnish with the chèvre and serve warm or at room temperature.

6 to 8 portions

NOTATIONS

CASA DE PEDRO SALAD

This Venezuelan-style salad is lush with avocado, tomatoes, and black beans. Lavished with a zippy cilantro vinaigrette, it's a star-spangled South American treat!

1 large head green leaf lettuce, broken into bite-size pieces
2 medium-size tomatoes, cut into 1-inch chunks
1 Haas avocado, pitted, peeled, and cut into 3/4-inch chunks
1 cup canned black beans, rinsed and drained
1/4 cup pepita seeds, toasted

Cilantro Vinaigrette:
salt and freshly ground pepper to taste
1 large clove garlic, smashed
1 tablespoon hot pepper jelly
1/4 cup finely chopped cilantro
2 tablespoons white wine vinegar
1/3 cup extra-virgin olive oil

1. Heap the lettuce in a large bowl. Add the tomatoes, avocado, black beans, and pepita seeds.

2. In a separate small bowl, whisk together the salt, pepper, garlic, hot pepper jelly, cilantro, vinegar, and oil until thick.

3. When ready to serve, remove the garlic from the dressing. Pour the vinaigrette over the salad, toss gently until evenly combined, and present.

6 portions

BRAZILIAN BEAN SALAD

NOTATIONS

Bean salads are in vogue. Not only are they delicious, they have the added benefit of being nutritious. This easy-to-prepare version showcases cannellini beans—one of my very favorites—teeming with a host of chopped vegetables—tomatoes, red and green peppers, and onions. Napped in a cilantro-laced vinaigrette, this dish has become a family favorite.

2 (14-ounce) cans cannellini beans, rinsed and drained
2 large plum tomatoes, chopped
1/2 large green pepper, chopped
1/2 large red pepper, chopped
1/2 medium-size red onion, chopped

Cilantro Vinaigrette:
salt and freshly ground pepper to taste
1 clove garlic, smashed
3 tablespoons finely chopped cilantro
1/4 cup chopped Italian parsley
3 tablespoons red wine vinegar
1/4 cup extra-virgin olive oil

1. Put the beans in a medium-size bowl. Add the tomatoes, peppers, and onion.

2. In a separate small bowl, whisk together the salt, pepper, garlic, cilantro, parsley, vinegar, and oil.

3. Pour the dressing over the salad, toss well, and let sit at room temperature for at least 30 minutes and as much as 2 hours to marinate.

4. When ready to serve, remove the garlic from the salad and present.

6 to 8 portions

NOTATIONS

MEDITERRANEAN CHICKPEA SALAD

This salad is gourmet comfort food. Chickpeas are cozied with Kalamata olives, roasted pepper, sun-dried tomatoes, and almonds. Dressed in a lemon vinaigrette, this makes a distinctive addition to barbecues and totes well to picnics. It's sure to become a permanent part of your repertoire.

3 cups canned chickpeas, rinsed and drained
1 large roasted red pepper, cut into 1/2-inch pieces
1/2 cup chopped, pitted Kalamata olives
1/2 cup chopped sun-dried tomatoes
1/3 cup slivered almonds, toasted
2 tablespoons capers

Lemon Vinaigrette:
salt and freshly ground pepper to taste
1 large clove garlic, smashed
1/4 cup chopped Italian parsley
1/4 cup lemon juice
1/2 cup extra-virgin olive oil

1. Put the chickpeas in a large bowl. Add the roasted pepper, olives, sun-dried tomatoes, almonds, and capers.

2. In a separate small bowl, whisk together the salt, pepper, garlic, parsley, lemon juice, and oil.

3. Pour the vinaigrette over the salad, toss well until evenly coated, and let marinate at room temperature for 1 to 2 hours. When ready to serve, remove the garlic from the salad and present.

5 to 6 portions

CHICKPEA AND PARSLEY SALAD

NOTATIONS

This is akin to the infamous Middle Eastern tabbouli salad. Chickpeas replace the bulgur, which is then surrounded by lush amounts of chopped mint and parsley. I like to serve this with grilled lamb.

14-ounce can chickpeas, rinsed and drained
2/3 cup finely chopped scallions
2 cups lightly packed, finely chopped curly parsley
3 tablespoons finely chopped mint

Lemon Vinaigrette:
salt and freshly ground pepper to taste
1/2 teaspoon ground cumin
2 tablespoons lemon juice
1/4 cup extra-virgin olive oil

1. Put the chickpeas in a medium-size bowl. Add the scallions, parsley, and mint.

2. In a separate small bowl, whisk together the salt, pepper, cumin, lemon juice, and oil.

3. Pour the vinaigrette over the salad, toss well until evenly mixed, and serve at room temperature.

4 portions

BEANS AU PISTOU

NOTATIONS

Pistou is the French counterpoint to pesto. It's a puréed blend of basil, garlic, extra-virgin olive oil, and sometimes Parmesan cheese. I've taken the liberty of adding lemon to boost the flavor. This fragrant sauce is splendid over this mixed bean medley.

3 cups shelled edamame, steamed
3 cups canned cannellini beans, rinsed and drained
3/4 pound green beans, cut into 1-inch lengths, steamed until tender-crisp, about 5 minutes
1/2 cup thinly sliced scallions
salt to taste

Pistou:
1 cup firmly packed basil
salt to taste
2 large cloves garlic, crushed
1/4 cup finely grated Parmigiano-Reggiano cheese
1 teaspoon finely grated lemon zest
1 tablespoon lemon juice
1/2 cup extra-virgin olive oil

1. Put the beans in a large bowl. Add the scallions and season with salt.

2. Put the basil, salt, garlic, cheese, lemon zest, and lemon juice in the bowl of a food processor and grind to a paste.

3. With the motor running, add the oil in a slow, steady stream until completely incorporated. Remove the pistou from the processor and pour it over the bean mixture. Toss well until evenly coated and serve at room temperature.

6 to 8 portions

SUCCOTASH

Succotash, an old-fashioned favorite, is bright, fresh, and hugely satisfying in this new-wave version. The beautiful simplicity of corn and cucumber combined with edamame, the fashionable Asian soy bean, basks in the glory of an herbed-lemon vinaigrette.

NOTATIONS

4 cups cooked corn kernels
2 cups shelled edamame, steamed
2 1/2 cups diced English cucumber (cut into 1/2-inch pieces)
4 scallions, thinly sliced

Herbed-Lemon Vinaigrette:
salt and freshly ground pepper to taste
2 tablespoons finely chopped dill
2 tablespoons finely chopped mint
1/4 cup chopped Italian parsley
3 tablespoons lemon juice
6 tablespoons extra-virgin olive oil

1. Put the corn, edamame, cucumber, and scallions in a large bowl.

2. In a separate small bowl, whisk together the salt, pepper, herbs, lemon juice, and oil.

3. Pour the dressing over the salad, toss well, and serve at room temperature.

6 to 8 portions

NOTATIONS

POTATOES AND GREEN BEANS NIÇOISE

This bright potato salad pairs spuds with garden fresh green beans and lush roasted red peppers. All is napped in a savory Dijon vinaigrette defined by Mediterranean flavors. This makes me salivate, it's so delicious!

1 1/2 pounds red-skinned potatoes, cut into 1-inch chunks
3/4 pound green beans, snapped in half and steamed until tender-crisp, about 5 minutes
2 roasted red peppers, cut into 3/4-inch pieces
1/2 cup thinly sliced scallions

Dijon Vinaigrette:
salt and freshly ground pepper to taste
1 large clove garlic, smashed
2 tablespoons Dijon mustard
1 teaspoon dried basil
1/4 cup chopped Italian parsley
2 tablespoons capers
2 tablespoons sherry vinegar
1/3 cup extra-virgin olive oil

1. Boil the potatoes in salted water until fork tender, about 10 to 15 minutes. Drain well and transfer to a large bowl.

2. Add the green beans, roasted peppers, and scallions to the potatoes.

3. In a separate small bowl, whisk together the salt, pepper, garlic, Dijon, basil, parsley, capers, vinegar, and oil until thick and creamy.

4. Pour the dressing over the vegetables, toss well, and let marinate for 30 minutes and as much as 2 hours. When ready to serve, remove the garlic from the salad and present.

6 or more portions

GREEN BEANS, WALNUTS, AND TOMATOES WITH WALNUT VINAIGRETTE

NOTATIONS

This colorful salad teams garden fresh green beans with juicy, sweet tomatoes and toasted walnuts. The rich-flavored walnut oil vinaigrette perfumes the salad, giving it an added dimension.

14 cups bite-size pieces red leaf lettuce
1/2 pound green beans, steamed until tender-crisp, about 5 minutes
12 cherry or large grape tomatoes, halved
1/2 cup coarsely chopped walnuts, toasted

Walnut Oil Vinaigrette:
salt and freshly ground pepper to taste
1 clove garlic, smashed
1 tablespoon Dijon mustard
2 tablespoons white wine vinegar
1/4 cup walnut oil
2 tablespoons olive oil (not extra-virgin)

1. Heap the lettuce in a large bowl. Add the green beans, tomatoes, and walnuts.

2. In a separate small bowl, whisk together the salt, pepper, garlic, Dijon, vinegar, and oils until thick and creamy.

3. When ready to serve, remove the garlic from the dressing. Pour the vinaigrette over the salad, toss well, and serve.

4 to 6 portions

TUSCAN WHITE BEAN SALAD

NOTATIONS

This white bean salad is host to a mélange of roasted ingredients—red peppers, tomatoes, and prosciutto. Roasting the different components concentrates and intensifies their flavor, making for a richer, more toothsome dish.

1 pint grape tomatoes, halved
extra-virgin olive oil for seasoning
salt
2 ounces thinly sliced prosciutto
4 1/2 cups canned cannellini beans, rinsed and drained
1 large roasted red pepper, cut into 3/4-inch pieces

Lemon-Balsamic Vinaigrette:
salt and freshly ground pepper to taste
1 clove garlic, smashed
2 teaspoons finely grated lemon zest
1 tablespoon lemon juice
1 tablespoon balsamic vinegar
1/4 cup extra-virgin olive oil

1. Roast the tomatoes. Preheat the oven to 300°. Spread the tomatoes out in a single layer on a rimmed baking sheet. Drizzle with olive oil and season with salt. Roast for 1 hour. (This may be done up to 8 hours in advance and stored covered at room temperature.)

2. Roast the prosciutto. Preheat the oven to 400°. Line a baking pan with parchment paper. Lay the slices of prosciutto on the parchment. Roast for 10 minutes until crisp and golden. Let cool, then coarsely chop.

3. Put the beans in a large bowl. Add the roasted tomatoes (and any accumulated pan juices) and roasted pepper.

4. In a separate small bowl, whisk together the salt, pepper, garlic, lemon zest, lemon juice, vinegar, and oil.

5. Pour the dressing over the bean mixture, tossing until evenly combined. Let marinate at room temperature for 30 minutes (and as much as 2 hours), for flavors to blend.

6. When ready to serve, remove the garlic from the salad. Garnish with the prosciutto, mix, and present.

6 portions

WALDORF-STYLE BULGUR SALAD

NOTATIONS

Bulgur, or cracked wheat, is a grain native to Middle Eastern cuisines. It forms the background for this lush Waldorf-style salad that's jam-packed with red grapes, celery, pecans, and raisins, and accented with sparkling, jewel-like pomegranate seeds. This makes a lovely, warm weather luncheon salad.

1 cup bulgur
1 1/2 cups boiling water
1 cup halved red seedless grapes
1 cup diced celery
1/4 cup diced red onion
generous 1/4 cup raisins
1/2 cup finely chopped pecans, toasted
1/4 cup pomegranate seeds
1/4 cup chopped Italian parsley

Balsamic Vinaigrette:
3/4 to 1 teaspoon salt (depending on taste)
freshly ground pepper to taste
2 tablespoons balsamic vinegar
6 tablespoons extra-virgin olive oil

1. Put the bulgur in a large bowl. Pour the boiling water over the bulgur and let stand for 1 hour until the water is absorbed. Fluff the bulgur with a fork.

2. Add the grapes, celery, red onion, raisins, pecans, pomegranate seeds, and parsley to the bulgur and mix until evenly combined.

3. In a separate small bowl, whisk together the salt, pepper, vinegar, and oil.

4. Pour the vinaigrette over the salad, toss well, and serve.

6 portions

NOTATIONS

WALNUT-CRACKED WHEAT SALAD

Walnuts are the quintessential ingredient in this bulgur salad that's reminiscent of tabbouli. Brimming with chopped parsley and scallions, the bright flavors of this walnut-whole wheat medley are uncommonly good.

1 cup bulgur
1 1/2 cups boiling water
1 1/2 cups finely chopped curly parsley
1 cup finely chopped walnuts, toasted
1/2 cup thinly sliced scallions
2/3 cup dried cranberries

Walnut Vinaigrette:
salt and freshly ground pepper to taste
1/4 cup lemon juice
1/4 cup walnut oil
2 tablespoons olive oil (not extra-virgin)

1. Put the bulgur in a large mixing bowl. Pour the boiling water over the bulgur and let stand for 1 hour until the water is absorbed. Fluff the bulgur with a fork.

2. Add the parsley, walnuts, scallions, and cranberries to the bulgur and mix well.

3. In a separate small bowl, whisk together the salt, pepper, lemon juice, and oils.

4. Pour the vinaigrette over the salad and toss well until evenly mixed. Serve at room temperature.

6 to 8 portions

COUSCOUS SALAD

NOTATIONS

Pre-toasting the couscous in this recipe lends a nutty quality to the dish. The toasted grain is replete with figs, pistachio nuts, and feta cheese, creating a most memorable salad.

1 cup Israeli couscous
1 1/4 cups water
12 dried Black Mission figs (stems removed), halved
heaping 1/3 cup shelled pistachio nuts
4 ounces feta cheese, crumbled

Lemon Vinaigrette:
1/2 teaspoon salt
freshly ground pepper to taste
1/4 cup chopped Italian parsley
2 tablespoons lemon juice
5 tablespoons extra-virgin olive oil

1. Toast the couscous. Preheat the oven to 350°. Spread the couscous out in a single layer on a rimmed baking sheet. Bake in the oven for 10 to 12 minutes until lightly golden. (This may be done up to 24 hours in advance and stored in an air-tight container.)

2. In a medium saucepan, bring the water to a boil. Stir in the couscous, cover, remove from the heat, and let sit for 25 minutes. Fluff with a fork.

3. While the couscous is steeping, whisk together the salt, pepper, parsley, lemon juice, and oil in a small bowl.

4. Pour the vinaigrette over the cooked couscous, stirring until evenly incorporated.

5. Add the figs, pistachios, and feta to the couscous, mix well, and serve.

4 portions

WHEATBERRY SALAD

NOTATIONS

Wheatberries are a whole grain. They're actually wheat without the husk. They boast a wholesome, nutty taste and slightly crunchy texture. Winter wheatberries are preferable as they don't get mushy when cooked. This hearty salad showcases a wheatberry base that's chock full of dried figs, craisins, and pecans. It makes an especially great companion to grilled meats and chicken.

1 cup winter wheatberries
salt to taste
1/2 cup dried cranberries
10 dried Calimyrna figs (stems removed), quartered
1/2 cup coarsely chopped pecans, toasted
1/2 cup thinly sliced scallions
2 tablespoons balsamic vinegar
6 tablespoons extra-virgin olive oil

1. Put the wheatberries in a medium-size saucepan with 3 cups of salted water. Bring to a boil, lower the heat, and simmer for about 45 minutes until the grain is soft. Drain well and transfer to a large bowl.

2. Add the cranberries, figs, pecans, and scallions.

3. In a separate small bowl, whisk together salt to taste, balsamic vinegar, and oil.

4. Pour the dressing over the salad, mix well until evenly combined, and serve warm or at room temperature.

6 portions

HEARTY SALADS

BACON, EGGS, AND TOAST

NOTATIONS

This is like breakfast in a bowl. Bacon, hard-boiled eggs, and French bread croutons team up in this stellar salad. Napped in a zesty, smoky-flavored mayonnaise, it's sure to get your attention.

1/2 pound French bread, cut into 1-inch cubes, lightly toasted
1/2 pound thick-sliced bacon, cooked until crisp and coarsely chopped
4 hard-boiled eggs, coarsely chopped

Dressing:
1/2 cup mayonnaise
salt and freshly ground pepper to taste
1 tablespoon Dijon mustard
1/2 teaspoon Worcestershire sauce
1/2 teaspoon smoked paprika
1 1/2 tablespoons heavy cream
2 tablespoons white wine vinegar

1. Heap the toasted bread in a large bowl. Add the bacon and eggs.

2. In a separate small bowl, mix the mayonnaise, salt, pepper, Dijon, Worcestershire, paprika, and heavy cream until evenly blended. Whisk in the vinegar.

3. Pour the dressing over the bread mixture, toss until evenly coated, and serve.

6 portions

CHOPPED COBB SALAD

NOTATIONS

Chopped salads are most fashionable. They're jam-packed with a myriad of tastes and textures. The layers of chopped ingredients in this classic—iceberg lettuce, tomato, bacon, hard-boiled egg, and blue cheese—are embellished with a dreamy, creamy avocado dressing. This is a gourmet's delight.

1 large head iceberg lettuce, chopped
2 large tomatoes, chopped
6 slices bacon, cooked until crisp and chopped
3 hard-boiled eggs, chopped
1/2 cup crumbled blue cheese

Avocado Dressing:
1 ripe Haas avocado, pitted, peeled, and cut into chunks
1/2 cup mayonnaise
1/4 cup buttermilk
salt and freshly ground pepper to taste
1 small clove garlic, crushed
dash of Worcestershire sauce
2 tablespoons red wine vinegar

1. Arrange the lettuce on individual plates. Adorn each portion with tomato, bacon, and egg. Garnish each with the crumbled blue cheese.

2. Put the avocado in the bowl of a food processor. Add the mayonnaise, buttermilk, salt, pepper, garlic, Worcestershire, and vinegar. Purée until smooth.

3. Top each salad with a generous dollop of dressing and serve.

4 to 6 portions

CHICKEN SALAD VÉRONIQUE

NOTATIONS

This is no ordinary, hum-drum chicken salad. It glistens with tender, moist chicken, juicy grapes, toasted pecans, and celery and sports a honey-mustard mayonnaise. This blue-ribbon winner makes a significant statement at the buffet table and totes well to picnics and barbecues.

2 whole medium-size chicken breasts (bone-in with skin), split in half
1 tablespoon olive oil (not extra-virgin)
salt and freshly ground pepper to taste
1 1/4 cups halved red grapes
1/2 cup coarsely chopped pecans, toasted
1/4 cup craisins
1 cup chopped celery, cut into 3/4-inch chunks
1/2 cup chopped red onion

Honey-Mustard Mayonnaise:
1/4 cup mayonnaise
salt and freshly ground pepper to taste
2 tablespoons Dijon mustard
2 tablespoons honey
1 tablespoon dark brown sugar

1. Preheat the oven to 375°. Put the chicken breasts on a parchment-lined, rimmed baking pan. Rub with oil and season with salt and pepper.

2. Roast for 40 to 45 minutes, until the chicken is just cooked. Remove from the oven and tent the chicken with foil for 10 minutes. (This allows the juices to redistribute in the chicken and makes for moister meat.) Set aside until cool enough to handle.

3. Remove the skin and bones from the chicken. Cut into 3/4-inch chunks and transfer to a large bowl.

4. Add the grapes, pecans, craisins, celery, and onion to the chicken. Mix until ingredients are evenly combined.

5. In a separate small bowl, whisk together the mayonnaise, salt, pepper, Dijon, honey, and brown sugar until smooth.

6. Pour the mayonnaise over the chicken salad, toss well until evenly coated, and serve.

6 portions

MANGO CHICKEN SALAD

NOTATIONS

Mango is the key ingredient that separates this chicken salad from all others. The Indian-inspired flavors of curry and chutney take center stage in this lively, fruity, and complex mélange. It's important to use homemade chutney—the jarred version is lackluster in comparison!

2 whole medium-size chicken breasts (bone-in with skin), split in half
1 tablespoon olive oil (not extra-virgin)
salt and freshly ground pepper to taste
2 ripe mangoes, peeled, pitted, and cut into 3/4-inch cubes (You may substitute frozen mango, thawed—you'll need about 2 cups.)
1 medium-size red pepper
1/2 cup thinly sliced scallions
1/2 cup cashew nuts, toasted

Curried-Chutney Mayonnaise:
3/4 cup mayonnaise
1/2 cup Mango Chutney (recipe follows)
salt and freshly ground pepper to taste
1 tablespoon curry powder
1 tablespoon Dijon mustard
2 tablespoons lemon juice

1. Preheat the oven to 375°. Put the chicken breasts on a parchment-lined, rimmed baking pan. Rub with oil and season with salt and pepper.

2. Roast for 40 to 45 minutes, until the chicken is just cooked. Remove from the oven and tent the chicken with foil for 10 minutes. (This allows the juices to redistribute in the chicken and makes for moister meat.) Set aside until cool enough to handle.

3. Remove the skin and bones from the chicken. Cut into 3/4-inch cubes and transfer to a large bowl.

4. Add the mangoes, red pepper, scallions, and cashews to the chicken. Mix until evenly combined.

5. In a separate small bowl, mix the mayonnaise, chutney, salt, pepper, curry powder, Dijon, and lemon juice until smooth and creamy.

6. Pour the dressing over the chicken salad, mix well, and serve.

8 portions

NOTATIONS

Mango Chutney:

2 ripe mangoes, peeled, pitted, and cut into 1/2-inch cubes (or frozen mango, thawed. You'll need 2 cups.)
1 medium-size yellow onion, chopped
1/3 cup raisins
1/2 small red pepper, diced
1 cup lightly packed dark brown sugar
1/3 cup white vinegar
1 large clove garlic, crushed
1 tablespoon coarsely grated gingerroot
1/8 teaspoon cayenne pepper
salt to taste

Put all of the ingredients in a large saucepan. Bring to a boil, lower the heat, and simmer until thick, about 30 minutes, stirring occasionally. Let cool, then pack into containers. Store in the refrigerator. This will keep for 4 to 6 weeks.

2 1/2 cups of chutney

CRAB SALAD

This glorious warm weather crab salad sparkles with a colorful mix of tomatoes, cucumber, scallions, and avocados. Tossed with a tarragon-mustard vinaigrette, it's cool, fresh, and vibrant. This is fabulous party fare.

NOTATIONS

1 pound King Crab meat from legs or fresh chunk crabmeat, cut into 3/4-inch chunks
4 hard-boiled eggs, coarsely chopped
3 cups halved cherry or grape tomatoes
1 English cucumber, cut into 3/4-inch chunks
2 Haas avocados, pitted, peeled, and coarsely chopped
4 scallions, cut into 1/2-inch long pieces

Tarragon Vinaigrette:
salt and freshly ground pepper to taste
1 1/2 tablespoons Dijon mustard
1 1/2 teaspoons dried tarragon
2 tablespoons finely chopped Italian parsley
1 tablespoon capers
3 tablespoons tarragon vinegar
2/3 cup olive oil (not extra-virgin)

1. Mound the crabmeat on a large platter. Add the eggs, tomatoes, cucumber, avocados, and scallions.

2. In a small bowl, whisk together the salt, pepper, Dijon, tarragon, parsley, capers, vinegar, and oil until thick and creamy.

3. Drizzle the dressing over the salad, toss gently, and serve.

6 to 8 portions

NOTATIONS

LOBSTER, CORN, AND TOMATO SALAD

This quintessential summer salad celebrates the bounty of the season. Sweet, garden-fresh tomatoes and corn are paired with succulent lobster and then tossed with a blue cheese dressing. The perfectly balanced symphony of flavors is sure to become your go-to specialty dish.

1 1/2 pounds cooked lobster meat, cut into 3/4-inch chunks
1 pint cherry or grape tomatoes, halved
3 cups cooked corn kernels (about 4 ears corn)
4 scallions, chopped into 1/2-inch lengths

Blue Cheese Vinaigrette:
salt and freshly ground pepper to taste
3 tablespoons lemon juice
2/3 cup extra-virgin olive oil
1/2 cup crumbled blue cheese

1. Put the lobster in a large bowl. Add the tomatoes, corn, and scallions.

2. In a separate small bowl, whisk together the salt, pepper, lemon juice, and olive oil. Stir in the blue cheese.

3. Pour the dressing over the salad and toss gently until evenly coated. Serve at room temperature.

6 portions

SHRIMP, MANGO, AND CUCUMBER SALAD

NOTATIONS

This colorful trio of ingredients—coral-hued shrimp, orange mango, and green cucumber—sports an Asian-inspired, ginger-lime vinaigrette punctuated with cilantro. Light and refreshing, this makes the perfect luncheon repast.

1 pound large shrimp, poached
2 ripe mangoes, peeled, pitted, and cut into bite-size chunks
1/2 English cucumber, cut into 3/4-inch chunks
1 small red onion, thinly sliced

Ginger-Lime Vinaigrette:
salt and freshly ground pepper to taste
1 tablespoon dark brown sugar
1 tablespoon Asian fish sauce
1 1/2 tablespoons grated gingerroot
1/4 cup chopped cilantro
1 teaspoon finely grated lime zest
3 tablespoons lime juice
1/4 cup olive oil (not extra-virgin)

1. Put the shrimp in a large bowl. Add the mangoes, cucumber, and onion.

2. In a separate small bowl, whisk together the salt, pepper, brown sugar, fish sauce, ginger, cilantro, lime zest, lime juice, and oil.

3. Pour the vinaigrette over the shrimp mixture, toss well until evenly coated, and serve.

4 to 6 portions

NOTATIONS

MEDITERRANEAN SHRIMP SALAD

Green leaf lettuce is host to grilled shrimp and tender artichoke hearts which is lavished in a zesty, lemon vinaigrette. This main-dish salad is simple, elegant, and most delicious.

1 3/4 pounds raw extra-large shrimp, shelled
extra-virgin olive oil
salt and freshly ground pepper to taste
14 cups bite-size pieces green leaf lettuce
14-ounce can artichoke hearts, rinsed, drained, and quartered

Lemon Vinaigrette:
salt and freshly ground pepper to taste
1 clove garlic, smashed
1/2 teaspoon anchovy paste
2 tablespoons chopped Italian parsley
1 1/2 tablespoons capers
3 tablespoons lemon juice
9 tablespoons (1/2 cup plus 1 tablespoon) extra-virgin olive oil

1. Skewer the shrimp. Drizzle with olive oil and season with salt and pepper.

2. Grill over hot coals, 4 inches from the heat source, about 2 minutes per side, until shrimp turn pink and are lightly charred.

3. Heap the lettuce in a large bowl. Add the shrimp and artichoke hearts.

4. In a separate small bowl, whisk together the salt, pepper, garlic, anchovy paste, parsley, capers, lemon juice, and oil.

5. When ready to serve, remove the garlic from the dressing. Pour the vinaigrette over the salad, toss well until evenly coated, and serve at once.

4 portions

SHRIMP ROLLS DECONSTRUCTED

NOTATIONS

Related to the fashionable lobster roll, this stellar version is just as glamorous. It's plentiful with shrimp, avocado, and celery, napped with a lemon mayonnaise, and garnished with squares of puff pastry. It's a sumptuous summer dish or anytime delight.

1/2 pound frozen puff pastry, thawed
2 pounds shelled shrimp, cooked and coarsely chopped
1 1/3 cups diced celery
2 Haas avocados, pitted, peeled, and cut into 3/4-inch pieces
1 cup mayonnaise
2 teaspoons Dijon mustard
3 tablespoons finely grated lemon zest
Boston lettuce

1. Preheat the oven to 400°. Grease a baking pan.

2. Cut the puff pastry in half; then cut each half into 4 equal pieces. Place on the baking pan and prick the pastry with a fork.

3. Bake for 15 minutes until golden. Set aside.

4. In a large bowl, combine the shrimp, celery, and avocados.

5. In a separate small bowl, mix the mayonnaise, Dijon, and lemon zest until evenly blended.

6. Add the mayonnaise to the shrimp and mix until evenly combined.

7. To serve, line individual plates with lettuce leaves. Mound the shrimp salad on the lettuce and garnish with a piece of puff pastry.

6 to 8 portions

LARB GAI

NOTATIONS

Larb Gai is the classic sautéed Thai ground chicken salad. I've taken the liberty of using ground turkey to add more depth of flavor to this spicy composition that's fragrant with chili paste, basil, and cilantro.

1 tablespoon Asian fish sauce
1 tablespoon dark brown sugar
1 large clove garlic, crushed
1 1/2 tablespoons grated gingerroot
grated zest and juice of 1 lime
1 tablespoon olive oil (not extra-virgin)
1 1/4 pounds ground turkey
salt and freshly ground pepper to taste
1 small red onion, thinly sliced
2 teaspoons Thai chili paste (or more to taste)
2 scallions, chopped
1/4 cup julienned basil
2 to 3 tablespoons chopped cilantro
shredded iceberg lettuce

1. In a small bowl, combine the fish sauce, brown sugar, garlic, ginger, lime zest, and lime juice.

2. Heat the oil in a wok. Add the turkey and break it up into small pieces. Season with salt and pepper.

3. As the turkey begins to brown, add the above fish sauce mixture, and continue to stir-fry until it is cooked through.

4. Add the onion and chili paste and stir-fry for 1 minute more. Remove from the heat and stir in the scallions, basil, and cilantro. Serve warm atop a bed of shredded lettuce.

4 portions

FINALES

Desserts are the extravagant, indulgent, cloying endings to meals, gatherings, and occasions. They are meant to be rich, decadent, and sinful, to satisfy that deep inner craving for sweets, and to be memorable down to the last mouthful. They should be tempting and seductive, romancing the senses with their appearance, aroma, and taste. Whether it's a delectable fruit crisp or an intense chocolate experience, make the dessert dazzle.

It is important not to compromise the experience by using low-fat or non-fat ingredients, or by substituting margarine in place of butter. I realize that some people are on restricted diets, but it's better to delight in one perfect spoonful than in a slice of mediocrity.

Charm your family and friends with a grand finale, making the stuff of which dreams are made!

FRUITS, PUDDINGS, AND CRISPS

GLAZED APPLES

NOTATIONS

Baked apples are a retro dessert. I've jazzed up the presentation by coating the apples with an aromatic, brown sugar glaze. It's guaranteed to keep you coming back for more.

4 Granny Smith apples
1/4 cup dark brown sugar
1/4 cup heavy cream
1 teaspoon five-spice powder

1. Preheat the oven to 375°.

2. Cut each apple in half through the core. Use a melon baller to scoop out the seed core from each half. Slice a thin layer from the bottom of each half to level the apples. Place the apples cored side up in a 9-inch square pan.

3. In a small bowl, combine the sugar, cream, and five-spice powder, stirring until well mixed. Spoon the mixture into the well of each apple and spread some over the top surface as well.

4. Bake for 30 minutes until brown and bubbly. Serve hot, warm, or at room temperature, garnished with scoops of vanilla ice cream or dollops of whipped cream.

4 or more portions

APRICOT CLAFOUTI

NOTATIONS

Clafouti is actually a fruit flan. It sports the same custard-like texture, but is also embedded with fragrant chunks of fruit. It's easy to assemble with outstanding results.

3 eggs
1/2 cup sugar
1 cup heavy cream
1/4 cup Amaretto
1 tablespoon vanilla
2/3 cup all-purpose flour
generous pinch of salt
2 (15-ounce) cans apricot halves, drained
1 1/2 tablespoons sugar mixed with 1/2 teaspoon cinnamon
confectioners' sugar for garnish

1. Preheat the oven to 350°. Grease a 9-inch deep-dish Pyrex pie pan.

2. In a large bowl with an electric mixer, beat the eggs and sugar until frothy. Add the cream, Amaretto, and vanilla and beat until evenly combined.

3. Add the flour and salt, beating until the batter is smooth and evenly mixed.

4. Pour a thin layer of batter into the prepared pan. Place the apricot halves, cut side down, on top of the batter in concentric circles. Sprinkle with the cinnamon-sugar mixture. Pour the remaining batter over the fruit.

5. Put the pie pan on a baking sheet—to catch any drips. Bake for 55 to 60 minutes until a toothpick inserted in the center comes out clean. Serve warm or at room temperature, dusted with confectioners' sugar.

6 to 8 portions

NOTATIONS

GLAZED APRICOTS

This dessert is so simple to prepare and so mouth-watering. Apricots are partnered with brown sugar, forming a lush, sweet-tart, glazed fruit that's served with a dollop of crème fraîche. It definitely has the yummy factor. (If fresh apricots are unavailable, use plums or pluots.)

6 ripe apricots, halved and pitted
1/4 cup dark brown sugar
crème fraîche for garnish

1. Preheat the broiler. Line a 9 x 13-inch baking pan with foil and grease the foil.

2. Place each apricot half, cut side up, in the pan. Spoon 1 teaspoon sugar on top of each half. Let sit for 30 minutes to allow the sugar to melt onto the flesh of the fruit.

3. Broil the apricots, 4 inches from the heat source, for 3 to 4 minutes until browned and bubbly. Remove the fruit to bowls, top each portion with a dollop of crème fraîche, and serve.

6 portions

BANANA BON BONS

Bananas are featured in the infamous chocolate-dipped fruit presentation that's the rage. Chunks of banana are coated in dark chocolate and encrusted with salted peanuts, creating a sweet-salty experience that's out of this world.

NOTATIONS

4 ounces semi-sweet chocolate, broken into small pieces
4 ounces bittersweet chocolate, broken into small pieces
2 large bananas, peeled and cut into 1 1/2-inch chunks
2/3 cup finely chopped, salted peanuts

1. Line a baking sheet with wax paper.

2. In the top of a double boiler over simmering water, heat the chocolates, stirring until melted and smooth. Remove from the heat.

3. Dip each banana chunk in the melted chocolate, rolling the pieces around to coat completely. Spear each chunk with a toothpick and then dip each piece in the peanuts, coating well.

4. Place each bon bon on the prepared baking sheet. Refrigerate for 30 minutes or up to 8 hours until the chocolate is set and you're ready to serve.

12 to 16 bon bons

BANANAS BROWN BETTY

NOTATIONS

A Brown Betty is a dessert consisting of fruit layered and topped with sweet, buttered bread crumbs. This rendition gives new definition to an old favorite with rum-macerated fruit and a brown sugar, cinnamon, and pecan crumb mixture. Serve it with crème fraîche or á la mode for total decadence.

4 large bananas, peeled and cut into 3/4-inch thick rounds
3 tablespoons dark rum
2 cups coarse bread crumbs from white sandwich bread (Prepare in a food processor.)
1/2 cup packed dark brown sugar
1/2 cup chopped pecans
1/4 teaspoon cinnamon
4 tablespoons unsalted butter, melted

1. Preheat the oven to 350°. Grease a 9-inch deep-dish pie pan.

2. In a bowl, combine the bananas and rum, mixing well until the fruit is evenly coated.

3. In a separate bowl, combine the bread crumbs, sugar, pecans, cinnamon, and butter. Stir until evenly mixed.

4. Sprinkle 3/4 of the crumb mixture over the bottom of the prepared pan. Top with the fruit and any accumulated juices. Spread the remaining crumbs over the bananas.

5. Bake for 40 to 45 minutes until the crumbs are brown. Serve warm or at room temperature garnished with dollops of crème fraîche or vanilla ice cream.

6 portions

DATE NUGGETS

NOTATIONS

Dates are the darlings of dried fruits. They're sweet like candy and are actually one-half sugar. Deglet dates are the most plentiful and are prized for their rich taste. These nuggets boast a pecan and mascarpone filling, perfumed with candied ginger. They're an irresistible treat.

3 dozen pitted Deglet dates
1/4 cup mascarpone cheese
2 tablespoons cream cheese, at room temperature
2 tablespoons finely chopped candied, crystallized ginger
2 tablespoons finely chopped pecans, toasted
2 tablespoons sugar mixed with 1/2 teaspoon cinnamon

1. Slice each date lengthwise on one side to butterfly it.

2. In a small bowl, combine the mascarpone, cream cheese, candied ginger, and pecans and mix until evenly blended.

3. Stuff each date with 1/2 teaspoon of the cheese mixture, then press gently to close slightly.

4. Roll each date in the cinnamon-sugar mixture, coating completely. Serve at room temperature. (These may be made 24 hours in advance and stored in the refrigerator. Return to room temperature to serve.)

3 dozen dates; allow 3 dates per person

NOTATIONS

FRUITS WITH RASPBERRY CREAM

This casual dessert is perfect for summertime entertaining. Colorful and refreshing, it's actually a raspberry-flavored mascarpone dip surrounded by an array of melons, berries, and stone fruits.

1 cup mascarpone cheese
1/4 cup heavy cream
1/4 cup raspberry preserves
an assortment of fruits (chunks of honeydew, cantaloupe, and pineapple; wedges of peaches, plums, and nectarines; cherries, strawberries, and blackberries)

1. In a bowl, mix the mascarpone with the cream and preserves until smooth.

2. Surround the dip with the cut fruit and present.

4 to 6 portions

CHOCOLATE CHIP RICOTTA CRÈME

NOTATIONS

I love to combine orange and chocolate—it's a sublime flavor pairing. This version of the whipped ricotta dessert showcases the cheese accented with chocolate chips, orange essence, and toasted almonds.

1 pound whole milk ricotta cheese
1 cup confectioners' sugar
1 tablespoon finely grated orange zest
2 tablespoons Grand Marnier
1/3 cup mini semi-sweet chocolate chips
2 tablespoons finely chopped almonds, toasted

1. Put the ricotta in a strainer suspended over a bowl and let drain for 1 hour.

2. In a bowl with an electric mixer, beat the ricotta, sugar, orange zest, and Grand Marnier until smooth and velvety. Mix in the chocolate chips. Refrigerate until ready to use—up to 24 hours.

3. To serve, scoop spoonfuls into bowls and sprinkle with the chopped almonds.

4 portions

NOTATIONS

COFFEE RICOTTA CRÈME

This easy-to-prepare, smooth, sweet ricotta dessert is a cross between a pudding and a Coeur á la crème. The creamy, whipped cheese is enhanced with coffee flavoring, making it the perfect after dinner treat.

1 pound whole milk ricotta cheese
2 tablespoons Kahlúa
1 tablespoon instant espresso coffee powder
3/4 cup confectioners' sugar

1. Put the ricotta in a strainer suspended over a bowl and let drain for 1 hour.

2. In a small bowl, combine the Kahlúa and espresso powder and mix well. Let sit for 10 minutes to allow the coffee to dissolve completely.

3. In a bowl with an electric mixer, beat the ricotta and sugar until smooth and velvety. Add the Kahlúa mixture and mix until evenly combined. Refrigerate until ready to use—up to 24 hours.

4. When ready to serve, scoop spoonfuls into bowls and top with sweetened whipped cream.

4 portions

LEMON COEUR Á LA CRÈME

Lemon is a refreshing, sparkling taste. This delicate, custard-like dessert is simply divine—it's perfumed with citrusy lemon and finished with a luscious raspberry sauce.

NOTATIONS

16 ounces mascarpone cheese
1/2 cup confectioners' sugar
1 tablespoon finely grated lemon zest
1 cup heavy cream
Raspberry Sauce (recipe follows)

1. In a bowl, combine the mascarpone, sugar, and lemon zest and mix well.

2. In a separate bowl, whip the cream until stiff peaks form.

3. Gently fold the whipped cream into the mascarpone mixture. Spoon the custard into cup-size ramekins and refrigerate at least 4 hours and as much as overnight to set.

4. Serve with the raspberry sauce spooned over the top.

6 portions

Raspberry Sauce:
1 1/2 cups fresh or frozen (defrosted) raspberries
3 tablespoons sugar

1. Put the raspberries in the bowl of a food processor and purée.

2. Sieve the purée through a fine strainer into a bowl to remove the seeds.

3. Stir in the sugar and refrigerate until serving time. (This may be made 24 hours in advance.)

NOTATIONS

MAPLE-PECAN RICOTTA CRÈME

Whipped ricotta is infused with maple syrup, brown sugar, and toasted pecans, encapsulating the flavors of pecan pie. It's smooth, sweet, and delicious.

1 pound whole milk ricotta cheese
1/3 cup packed dark brown sugar
3 tablespoons pure maple syrup
1 1/2 teaspoons vanilla
1/4 teaspoon cinnamon
1/3 cup chopped pecans, toasted

1. Put the ricotta in a strainer suspended over a bowl and let drain for 1 hour.

2. In a bowl with an electric mixer, beat the ricotta, brown sugar, maple syrup, vanilla, and cinnamon until smooth and velvety. Mix in the pecans. Refrigerate until ready to use—up to 24 hours.

3. To serve, scoop spoonfuls into bowls and present.

4 portions

ORANGE CREAMSICLE

This jazzed-up version of the retro ice cream pop is both refreshing and irresistible on the dog days of summer.

1 quart favorite vanilla ice cream
1/3 cup orange marmalade
1 1/2 tablespoons Grand Marnier

1. Scoop the ice cream into a large bowl and let soften slightly.

2. In a small bowl, mix the marmalade and liqueur. Add the mixture to the softened ice cream, stirring until evenly distributed.

3. Place in the freezer for at least 2 hours for the ice cream to harden. (This can be made as much as 2 days in advance.)

4. When ready to serve, scoop into bowls and present.

4 to 6 portions

NOTATIONS

APPLE KUGEL

NOTATIONS

Adding apples to the classic noodle pudding gives it a fruity dimension. It's almost like an apple pie and noodle pudding in one. It's absolutely delicious and makes a grand statement at the brunch table.

4 eggs, beaten
2/3 cup sugar
1 pint sour cream
1 teaspoon vanilla
1 teaspoon cinnamon
pinch of nutmeg
1/2 teaspoon salt
4 tablespoons unsalted butter, melted and cooled
2 cups buttermilk
12 ounces medium-size egg noodles
3 large Granny Smith apples, peeled, cored, quartered, and thinly sliced
1/2 cup golden raisins

1. Preheat the oven to 350°. Grease a 9 x 13-inch Pyrex baking pan.

2. In a large bowl, combine the eggs, sugar, sour cream, vanilla, cinnamon, nutmeg, and salt and mix well. Stir in the butter and buttermilk.

3. Boil the noodles in salted water for 5 minutes. Drain well and add to the custard mixture, stirring until evenly combined.

4. Add the apples and raisins and mix well. Turn the pudding into the prepared baking dish.

5. Bake for 45 to 60 minutes or until set and golden. Let the pudding sit for 10 minutes before cutting into pieces.

12 portions

APRICOT-WHITE CHOCOLATE BREAD PUDDING

NOTATIONS

Dried apricots, white chocolate, and candied ginger are the trademark ingredients that punctuate this lush bread pudding. Bursting with flavor, it's equally delicious served hot out of the oven, warm, or at room temperature.

3/4 pound day old soft Italian or French bread, cut into 1-inch chunks
4 eggs, beaten
1 quart whole milk
4 tablespoons unsalted butter, melted and cooled
1 cup light brown sugar
pinch of salt
1 teaspoon ground ginger
1/3 cup diced candied, crystallized ginger
1 1/2 cups chopped dried apricots
1 1/3 cups white chocolate chips

1. Preheat the oven to 350°. Grease a 9 x 13-inch Pyrex baking dish.

2. Put the bread in a large mixing bowl.

3. In a separate bowl, whisk together the eggs, milk, butter, sugar, salt, and ground ginger. Pour the custard over the bread chunks, mix well until evenly coated, and let sit for 20 minutes for the bread to absorb the liquid.

4. Stir in the candied ginger, apricots, and chocolate chips. Turn the pudding into the prepared pan.

5. Bake for 50 to 60 minutes until set and golden. Serve the pudding hot, warm, or at room temperature.

12 or more portions

PECAN STREUSEL BREAD PUDDING

NOTATIONS

Bread puddings are real comfort foods. This is THE DELUXE of bread puddings. It's actually a rich bread pudding encrusted with a pecan pie topping. What could be more sumptuous? It makes a grand statement at brunches, buffets, and dinner parties alike.

1 pound day old Italian bread, cut into 1-inch chunks
4 eggs, beaten
2 cups whole milk
2 cups heavy cream
1 1/2 teaspoons vanilla
1/2 cup sugar mixed with 1 teaspoon cinnamon
pinch of salt

Topping:
1/2 cup unsalted butter, at room temperature
1 cup firmly packed dark brown sugar
2 tablespoons dark corn syrup
1 1/4 cups coarsely chopped pecans

1. Preheat the oven to 350°. Grease a 9 x 13-inch Pyrex baking dish.

2. Put the bread in a large mixing bowl.

3. In a separate bowl, whisk together the eggs, milk, cream, vanilla, sugar mixture, and salt. Pour the custard over the bread chunks, mix well until evenly coated, and let sit for 20 minutes for the bread to absorb the liquid.

4. Turn the pudding into the prepared pan.

5. Prepare the topping. In a bowl with an electric mixer, cream the butter, sugar, and corn syrup. Mix in the pecans.

6. Distribute small spoonfuls of the topping evenly over the pudding, spreading it slightly with a knife. The top will not be completely covered with the praline topping.

7. Bake for 45 to 50 minutes until puffed and set. Serve hot, warm, or at room temperature. It's extravagant with dollops of whipped cream or vanilla ice cream.

12 or more portions

STICKY TOFFEE PUDDING

NOTATIONS

This classic English pudding is actually a sticky, sweet sponge cake laden with dates. This version is infused with the exotic flavor of candied ginger. Drizzled with a delectable caramel sauce, it's an especially sweet experience.

1 1/2 cups chopped, pitted dates
1 1/4 cups water
1 teaspoon baking soda
4 tablespoons unsalted butter, at room temperature
3/4 cup dark brown sugar
2 eggs
1 teaspoon vanilla
2 tablespoons minced candied, crystallized ginger
1 1/2 cups all-purpose flour
1 teaspoon baking powder
1/2 teaspoon salt
Caramel Sauce (recipe follows)
crème fraîche

1. Put the dates and water in a medium-size saucepan. Bring to a boil. Remove from heat and stir in the baking soda. The mixture will become foamy. Set aside and let cool.

2. Preheat the oven to 350°. Grease a 9-inch square baking pan.

3. In a large bowl with an electric mixer, cream the butter and sugar. Add the eggs, vanilla, and ginger and beat until fluffy.

4. Sift together the flour, baking powder, and salt. Add the dry ingredients to the batter, mixing until evenly blended.

5. Add the cooled date mixture, beating until evenly incorporated. Pour the batter into the prepared pan.

6. Bake for about 40 minutes until a toothpick inserted in the center comes out clean. Place on a rack to cool slightly; then serve with the warm caramel sauce poured over each portion. Garnish with a dollop of crème fraîche.

9 portions

NOTATIONS

Caramel Sauce:
4 tablespoons unsalted butter, at room temperature
1/2 cup heavy cream
1/2 cup dark brown sugar
1/2 teaspoon vanilla

1. Put the butter, cream, and sugar in a small saucepan and bring to a boil over medium heat, stirring constantly. Lower the heat and simmer for 5 minutes, stirring occasionally. Remove from the heat.

2. Stir in the vanilla. Pour the warm sauce over each serving of pudding. (The sauce may be made up to 24 hours in advance and refrigerated until needed. Reheat gently before serving.)

NOODLE PUDDING REVISITED

NOTATIONS

This updated version of the infamous pudding in my ***Uncommon Gourmet Cookbook*** is a family favorite. I've included it in the dessert section because it's so sweet and absolutely divine. However, it can also be presented as part of the main course or as a mainstay for brunch. It's über comfort food.

4 eggs, beaten
3/4 cup sugar mixed with 1 teaspoon cinnamon
1 1/2 pounds cottage cheese
1 pound sour cream
1 tablespoon vanilla
1/2 teaspoon salt
1/2 cup butter, melted and cooled
1 cup buttermilk
1 pound wide egg noodles

1. Preheat the oven to 350°. Grease an 11 x 13-inch baking pan.

2. In a large bowl, combine the eggs, sugar mixture, cottage cheese, sour cream, vanilla, and salt and mix well. Stir in the butter and buttermilk.

3. Boil the noodles in salted water for 5 minutes. Drain well and add to the custard mixture, stirring until evenly combined.

4. Turn the pudding into the prepared baking dish.

5. Bake for about 1 hour or until the pudding is set and golden. Let sit for 5 minutes before cutting into pieces. Serve hot, warm, or at room temperature.

12 or more portions

NOTATIONS

APPLE CRISP REVISITED

Revisiting an old classic has its rewards. This stepped-up version from my ***All-Occasion Cookbook*** is plumper with more apples. It also boasts a brown sugar-oatmeal crumb topping that's sure to put a smile on your face.

5 large Granny Smith apples, peeled, cored, and cut into 1-inch chunks
3 tablespoons sugar mixed with 1 teaspoon cinnamon
2 tablespoons all-purpose flour

Topping:
1 cup all-purpose flour
1/2 cup dark brown sugar
1/2 cup granulated sugar
1/2 teaspoon baking powder
1/8 teaspoon salt
1 1/2 teaspoons vanilla
6 tablespoons cold, unsalted butter, cut into 1/4-inch cubes
2/3 cup old-fashioned oats

1. Preheat the oven to 350°. Grease a 9-inch deep-dish pie pan.

2. In a large bowl, toss the apples with the cinnamon-sugar mixture and 2 tablespoons flour. Transfer to the prepared pie pan.

3. Prepare the crumb topping. In a separate large bowl, mix the flour, sugars, baking powder, and salt. Using a pastry blender or fork, add the vanilla and butter, and mix until the texture of coarse meal. Stir in the oats.

4. Cover the apples with the crumb mixture.

5. Bake for 45 to 50 minutes until golden. Serve hot, warm, or at room temperature.

8 or more portions

BLUEBERRY CRISP

NOTATIONS

There's no soggy crust in this bottomless blueberry pie! Piled high with blueberries and sporting a buttery, vanilla crumb topping, this crisp is the pick of summer's bounty.

Filling:
5 cups blueberries
1/3 cup sugar
3 tablespoons all-purpose flour

Crumb Topping:
1 cup all-purpose flour
3/4 cup sugar
1/2 cup cold unsalted butter, cut into small pieces
1 teaspoon vanilla

1. Preheat the oven to 350°. Grease a 9-inch deep-dish pie pan.

2. Heap the blueberries in the prepared pan. Sprinkle with the sugar and flour and mix well.

3. Make the crumb topping. In the bowl of a food processor, put the flour, sugar, butter, and vanilla. Pulse until the texture of coarse crumbs.

4. Using a fork to separate the clumps, distribute the crumb mixture evenly over the berries, coating generously.

5. Bake for 45 minutes until golden. Serve hot out of the oven, warm, or at room temperature with scoops of vanilla ice cream.

6 to 8 portions

MIXED BERRY CRISP

NOTATIONS

I just love crisps—they're easy to assemble and there's never a wet pastry crust! This crisp showcases a potpourri of lush berries crowned with a crunchy granola topping. This makes for heavenly indulgence.

5 cups mixed berries (blueberries, raspberries, and blackberries—I like to use one-half blueberries.)
1/4 cup sugar
2 tablespoons raspberry preserves, melted
1/3 cup all-purpose flour

Topping:
1/2 cup all-purpose flour
pinch of salt
3/4 cup light brown sugar
1/2 cup cold unsalted butter, cut into 1/4-inch cubes
3/4 cup old-fashioned oats
1/2 cup chopped almonds

1. Preheat the oven to 350°. Grease a 9-inch deep-dish pie pan.

2. In a large bowl, gently toss the berries with the sugar and preserves. Mix in the flour. Transfer the mixture to the prepared pan.

3. Make the topping. In a medium-size bowl, mix the flour, salt, and sugar. Using a pastry blender or fork, cut in the butter until the texture of coarse meal. Stir in the oats and almonds.

4. Cover the berries with the crumb topping.

5. Bake for 45 minutes until golden. Serve hot, warm, or at room temperature.

6 to 8 portions

COOKIES, BARS, AND BISCOTTI

ALMOND MACAROONS

NOTATIONS

Macaroons were a childhood holiday specialty. Now I enjoy these chewy, almond-infused morsels year round.

2 egg whites (from extra-large eggs)
1 teaspoon almond extract
1 1/4 cups sugar
1 1/2 cups finely ground almonds

1. Preheat the oven to 350°. Line 2 cookie sheets with parchment paper.

2. With an electric mixer, beat the egg whites and almond extract until frothy. Gradually add the sugar, 1 tablespoon at a time, beating until whites are glossy and form stiff peaks.

3. Gently fold in the ground almonds.

4. Drop the batter by heaping tablespoonfuls onto the prepared cookie sheets in 1 1/2-inch mounds, 2 inches apart.

5. Bake for 15 to 18 minutes until golden. Remove from the oven and transfer the cookies to a rack to cool.

16 cookies

ALMOND SUGAR COOKIES

NOTATIONS

Lots of butter, sugar, and almond flavoring make these a favorite cookie choice in our family.

1 cup unsalted butter, at room temperature
1 cup sugar
1 egg
1 teaspoon almond extract
2 1/2 cups all-purpose flour
1 1/2 teaspoons baking soda
1/4 teaspoon salt
granulated sugar for dipping
30 whole blanched almonds

1. In a large mixing bowl with an electric mixer, cream the butter and sugar until fluffy. Add the egg and almond extract and mix well.

2. Sift together the flour, baking soda, and salt and add to the batter. Mix until the dough is evenly blended. Refrigerate for 30 minutes.

3. Preheat the oven to 350°. Grease two baking sheets.

4. Using 1 1/2 tablespoonfuls of dough, roll into balls. With the palm of your hand, flatten the balls to form 2 1/4-inch rounds. Dip one side in sugar and place sugar side up on the prepared baking sheets, 2 inches apart. Impress an almond in the center of each cookie.

5. Bake for 10 to 12 minutes until lightly golden. Let the cookies sit on the baking sheets for 1 minute before removing them to racks to cool.

30 cookies

AMARETTO BON BONS

NOTATIONS

I absolutely love almond paste! It's the key ingredient in these dainty morsels. It's simply sugar and finely ground almonds, but it has a wonderful, chewy consistency and heavenly taste.

2 cups graham cracker crumbs
3/4 cup confectioners' sugar
1/4 cup almond paste, cut into small pieces
1/2 cup mascarpone cheese
2 tablespoons Amaretto
1 teaspoon vanilla
confectioners' sugar for coating

1. Put the graham crumbs, 3/4 cup confectioners' sugar, almond paste, mascarpone, Amaretto, and vanilla in the bowl of a food processor. Pulse until the mixture is smooth.

2. Remove the mixture from the bowl and wrap in plastic wrap. Refrigerate at least 4 hours and as much as overnight for dough to chill.

3. Using 1 tablespoonful of mixture, roll the dough into balls. Roll the balls in confectioners' sugar, coating completely. Store in the refrigerator; remove 30 minutes before serving.

about 28 bon bons

APRICOT-DATE FOGGIES

NOTATIONS

Akin to Oatmeal Foggies in my ***All-Occasion Cookbook***, these nuggets are even more sumptuous. Infused with dried fruits and nuts and scented with cinnamon, they're a popular cookie choice at XMAS.

1/2 cup unsalted butter, at room temperature
1/2 cup granulated sugar
1/2 cup packed dark brown sugar
3 tablespoons pure maple syrup
1 cup all-purpose flour
1 teaspoon baking soda
1/4 teaspoon salt
1 teaspoon cinnamon
1 cup old-fashioned oats
1/2 cup diced pitted dates
1/2 cup diced dried apricots
1/2 cup chopped pecans

1. Preheat the oven to 350°.

2. In a large bowl with an electric mixer, cream the butter, sugars, and maple syrup.

3. Add the flour, baking soda, salt, and cinnamon and mix well.

4. Add the oats, dates, apricots, and pecans, mixing until evenly blended. Using 1 1/2 tablespoonfuls of dough, form into balls. With the palm of your hand, flatten the balls to from 2-inch rounds. Place on ungreased cookie sheets, 2 inches apart.

5. Bake for 10 minutes. Let the cookies sit on the baking sheets for 3 minutes before removing them to racks to cool.

32 cookies

NOTATIONS

BROWN EDGE WAFERS

Golden around the edges as the name implies, these thin, crispy wafers are reminiscent of my very favorite childhood cookie. They're perfect for teatime, for dunking into milk, or simply for munching.

6 tablespoons olive oil (not extra-virgin)
1/2 cup sugar
1 egg, beaten
1 1/2 teaspoons vanilla
1 cup all-purpose flour
3/4 teaspoon baking powder
1/4 teaspoon salt

1. Preheat the oven to 350°. Grease two cookie sheets.

2. In a medium-size bowl, mix the oil and sugar. Stir in the egg and vanilla.

3. Add the flour, baking powder, and salt and mix well.

4. Using 1 tablespoonful of dough, drop the batter onto the cookie sheets forming circles, 2 inches apart.

5. Bake for 10 to 12 minutes until lightly golden around the edges. Let the cookies sit on the baking sheets for 1 minute before removing them to racks to cool.

2 dozen cookies

DANISH BUTTER COOKIES

These dainty, crispy wafers are scented with cardamom. Cardamom is a strong, fragrant spice. The aroma of ground cardamom is elusive—it has a whisper of ginger, coriander, and white pepper, lending a classic note to these cookies.

NOTATIONS

1/2 cup unsalted butter, at room temperature
3/4 cup packed light brown sugar
1 teaspoon vanilla
1/3 cup light cream
2 cups all-purpose flour
1/4 teaspoon baking soda
1/8 teaspoon salt
1/2 teaspoon ground cardamom
white sugar crystals

1. In a bowl with an electric mixer, cream the butter and sugar. Add the vanilla and cream and beat until fluffy.

2. Add the flour, baking soda, salt, and cardamom and mix until dough comes together. Transfer the dough to a piece of plastic wrap and form into a log, 9 inches long. Refrigerate the dough overnight.

3. Preheat the oven to 350°. Line two baking sheets with parchment paper.

4. With a thin, sharp knife, slice the dough into 1/4-inch thick rounds. Place on the prepared baking sheets, 2 inches apart. Sprinkle generously with white sugar crystals.

5. Bake for 12 to 14 minutes until the cookies are slightly sandy-colored around the edges. Remove the cookies to racks to cool completely. Note—the cookies will crisp as they cool.

3 dozen

MAPLE CORNMEAL COOKIES

NOTATIONS

These delicate, crispy-edged cookies strut a cornmeal base that's infused with the rich, smoky flavor of maple syrup. They're perfect for nibbling alongside bowls of ice cream.

1/2 cup unsalted butter, at room temperature
1/2 cup sugar
1 egg
2 tablespoons pure maple syrup
3/4 cup all-purpose flour
1/2 cup cornmeal
1/4 teaspoon salt

1. Preheat the oven to 350°. Line two baking sheets with parchment paper.

2. In a large bowl with an electric mixer, cream the butter and sugar until fluffy. Add the egg and maple syrup and mix well.

3. Add the flour, cornmeal, and salt and mix only until evenly combined.

4. Using 1 tablespoonful of dough, drop the batter onto the baking sheets, 2 inches apart.

5. Bake for 10 to 12 minutes until the edges are golden. Transfer the cookies to racks to cool completely.

34 cookies

CRANBERRY-NUT COOKIES

NOTATIONS

Dried cranberries provide that sweet-tart quality to these fragrantly spiced, chewy, nut-encrusted cookies. Fashioned with goodness, these cookies pack a punch.

1/2 cup unsalted butter, at room temperature
1/2 cup packed dark brown sugar
1/2 cup granulated sugar
1 egg
1 teaspoon vanilla
1 tablespoon grated orange zest
1 1/4 cups all-purpose flour
1/2 teaspoon baking soda
1/4 teaspoon salt
1 teaspoon cinnamon
1/2 teaspoon nutmeg
1/8 teaspoon ground cloves
1 cup dried cranberries
1 cup chopped walnuts

1. In a large bowl with an electric mixer, cream the butter and sugars until fluffy. Add the egg, vanilla, and orange zest and mix well.

2. Sift together the flour, baking soda, salt, cinnamon, nutmeg, and cloves and add to the batter, mixing well.

3. Add the cranberries and nuts, mixing until evenly incorporated. Place the dough in plastic wrap and refrigerate for 2 to 3 hours, and as much as overnight.

4. Preheat the oven to 375°. Line two baking sheets with parchment paper.

5. Using 1 1/2 tablespoonfuls of dough, form into balls. With the palm of your hand, flatten the balls to form 2-inch rounds. Place on the prepared cookie sheets, 2 inches apart.

6. Bake for 8 to 10 minutes until lightly browned around the edges. Let the cookies sit on the baking sheets for 3 minutes before removing them to racks to cool.

3 dozen

COFFEE-GINGER MERINGUES

NOTATIONS

Coffee and ginger have a curious affinity. This flavor combo elevates these melt-in-the-mouth clouds to fashionable heights. They disappear like soap bubbles! A word of caution—don't attempt to make these on a rainy or humid day, they'll never crisp!

3/4 cup sugar
1 tablespoon instant espresso coffee powder
1 teaspoon ground ginger
2 egg whites (from extra-large eggs), at room temperature

1. Preheat the oven to 225°. Line two baking sheets with parchment paper.

2. In a small bowl, combine the sugar, coffee, and ginger, mixing until evenly combined.

3. In a large bowl with an electric mixer, beat the egg whites until frothy. While beating on high, gradually add the sugar mixture. Continue beating for 5 minutes until the whites are stiff and glossy.

4. Using a rounded teaspoonful of the beaten whites, mound the batter onto the prepared baking sheets, 2 inches apart.

5. Bake for 1 hour. Transfer the meringues to racks to cool completely.

3 dozen meringues

INDIVIDUAL PAVLOVAS

NOTATIONS

Named after the famous Russian ballerina, Anna Pavlova, a Pavlova is a large meringue that's topped with whipped cream and fruit. I've modified this creation, making individual over-sized meringues and crowning them with vanilla ice cream and strawberry sauce. (Hint—don't attempt to make these on a rainy or humid day as they will never crisp. However, they can be made ahead and frozen.)

Strawberry Sauce:
1 quart strawberries, hulled and halved
2 tablespoons sugar

Put the strawberries in a bowl and sprinkle with the sugar. Let sit at room temperature for 3 to 4 hours (and up to 8 hours) for berries to release their juices and form a syrupy sauce.

Pavlovas:
3 egg whites (from extra-large eggs)
1½ teaspoons vanilla
¾ cup sugar

vanilla ice cream

1. Preheat the oven to 325°. Line two baking sheets with parchment paper.

2. In a bowl with an electric mixer, combine the egg whites and vanilla. Beat the whites until frothy; then gradually add the sugar 1 tablespoon at a time, beating constantly. Beat on the high setting for 7 to 8 minutes until the whites are stiff and glossy.

3. Drop large spoonfuls of the mixture onto the parchment paper and spread each mound into a 3-inch circle, leaving 2 inches between each Pavlova.

4. Bake for 1 to 1½ hours until crisp. Remove to a rack to cool completely.

5. When ready to serve, top each Pavlova with a scoop of vanilla ice cream and a large spoonful of strawberry sauce.

10 portions

NOTATIONS

THE ULTIMATE CHOCOLATE CHIP-OATMEAL COOKIES

These homespun cookies appeal to both chocolate lovers and oatmeal cookie fans alike—they're chewy, rich, and chunky with chocolate chips, making these the number one oatmeal cookie.

3/4 cup unsalted butter, at room temperature
3/4 cup firmly packed light brown sugar
1/4 cup granulated sugar
1 egg
2 teaspoons vanilla
1 cup all-purpose flour
3/4 teaspoon baking soda
1/4 teaspoon salt
1 teaspoon cinnamon
2 cups old-fashioned oats
1 cup semi-sweet chocolate chips

1. Preheat the oven to 350°. Line two baking sheets with parchment paper.

2. In a large bowl with an electric mixer, cream the butter and sugars until fluffy. Add the egg and vanilla and mix well.

3. Sift together the flour, baking soda, salt, and cinnamon and add to the batter, mixing well.

4. Stir in the oats and chips.

5. Using 1 1/2 tablespoonfuls of dough, drop the batter onto the baking sheets, 2 inches apart.

6. Bake for 10 to 12 minutes until golden. Let the cookies sit on the baking sheets for 2 to 3 minutes before removing them to racks to cool.

3 dozen

PECAN SANDIES

These cookies are the real McCoy. These buttery rich, pecan-encrusted, sweet treats are reminiscent of childhood favorites.

2 cups all-purpose flour
1 cup unsalted butter, cut into small pieces
1/2 cup sugar
1 1/2 teaspoons vanilla
1/4 teaspoon salt
1 cup chopped pecans
extra sugar for garnish

1. Put the flour, butter, 1/2 cup sugar, vanilla, and salt in the bowl of a food processor. Pulse until the mixture comes together. Add the nuts and pulse only until evenly incorporated.

2. Transfer the dough to a piece of wax paper and form into two logs, each 6 inches long. Wrap each log in plastic wrap and refrigerate overnight.

3. Preheat the oven to 350°.

4. Remove one log from the refrigerator and let sit for 2 minutes. Then using a thin, sharp knife, slice the dough into 1/4-inch thick rounds. Place on ungreased cookie sheets, 2 inches apart.

5. Bake for 15 minutes until golden around the edges. Let the cookies sit on the baking sheets for 1 minute, then remove to racks. While still warm, sprinkle generously with sugar. Let cool completely. Repeat the baking process with the second log of dough.

4 dozen cookies

NOTATIONS

PIGNOLI NUT COOKIES

NOTATIONS

These cookies are like the jewels found in the pastry shop in Boston's North End. They're crispy around the edges, chewy in the middle, and encrusted with pine nuts.

7-ounce tube almond paste, cut into small pieces
1 cup sugar
pinch of salt
2 egg whites
1/2 cup pine nuts

1. Preheat the oven to 300°. Line two baking sheets with parchment paper.

2. Put the almond paste, sugar, and salt in the bowl of a food processor and pulse until the texture of coarse meal.

3. Add the egg whites and pulse until the dough is smooth. Transfer the dough to a bowl. Stir in the nuts.

4. Using rounded tablespoonfuls of dough, drop the batter onto the baking sheets, 2 inches apart.

5. Bake for 16 to 18 minutes until lightly golden, rotating the baking sheets halfway through the baking time. Remove the parchment with the cookies to racks to cool for 15 minutes; then carefully peel the cookies from the parchment and put them on racks to cool completely.

30 cookies

PISTACHIO BUTTER COOKIES

These tea cookies boast the characteristics of a great shortbread—a buttery flavor and sandy texture. I've further gilded the lily by infusing them with almond essence and pistachio nuts.

NOTATIONS

1 cup unsalted butter, at room temperature
3/4 cup sugar
1 teaspoon almond extract
2 cups all-purpose flour
1/4 teaspoon salt
1 cup shelled pistachio nuts, chopped
confectioners' sugar for garnish

1. Preheat the oven to 350°.

2. In a large bowl with an electric mixer, cream the butter and sugar until fluffy. Add the extract and mix well.

3. Add the flour and salt and mix until the dough comes together. Stir in the nuts.

4. Using 1 tablespoonful of dough, roll into balls. With the palm of your hand, flatten the balls to form 2-inch rounds. Place on ungreased cookie sheets, 2 inches apart.

5. Bake for 10 to 12 minutes until golden around the edges. Let the cookies sit on the baking sheet for 1 minute before removing them to racks to cool. While still warm, dust the cookies with confectioners' sugar.

44 cookies

NOTATIONS

SPICE CRISPS

This cookie jar favorite is packed with homespun goodness. Scented with a potpourri of aromatic spices, no one can resist these crispy wafers.

1 cup unsalted butter, at room temperature
1 cup sugar
1 egg
2 1/2 cups all-purpose flour
1 1/2 teaspoons baking soda
1/2 teaspoon salt
1 1/4 teaspoons cinnamon
1 teaspoon ground ginger
1/4 teaspoon nutmeg
1/8 teaspoon ground cloves
white sugar crystals for dipping

1. In a large bowl with an electric mixer, cream the butter and sugar until fluffy. Add the egg and mix well.

2. Sift together the flour, baking soda, salt, and spices and add to the batter, mixing well. Refrigerate the dough for 30 minutes.

3. Preheat the oven to 350°. Grease two baking sheets.

4. Using 1 1/2 tablespoonfuls of dough, roll into balls. Using the palm of your hand, flatten the balls to form 2 1/4-inch rounds. Dip one side in white sugar crystals. Place sugar side up on the cookie sheets, 2 inches apart.

5. Bake for 10 to 12 minutes until lightly golden. Let the cookies sit on the baking sheets for 1 minute before removing them to racks to cool.

30 cookies

CHOCOLATE CHIP SHORTBREAD

NOTATIONS

Distinctively buttery, tender, and crumbly, the way a shortbread should be, these squares are scented with almond essence and dotted with chocolate chips.

1/2 cup unsalted butter, at room temperature
1/2 cup confectioners' sugar
1/2 teaspoon almond extract
1/4 cup cornstarch
1/4 teaspoon salt
3/4 cup all-purpose flour
1/4 cup mini semi-sweet chocolate chips

1. Preheat the oven to 300°. Line an 8-inch square pan with parchment paper, letting it overhang the pan on two opposite sides.

2. In a bowl with an electric mixer, cream the butter, sugar, and almond extract until fluffy. Add the cornstarch and salt and mix well.

3. Gradually add the flour, being careful not to overbeat the dough or it will get tough. Stir in the chocolate chips by hand.

4. Transfer the dough to the prepared pan and press it evenly into place to conform to the shape of the pan.

5. Bake for 45 to 50 minutes until pale golden. Using the parchment overhang, gently lift the shortbread out of the pan and place on a wooden board. While still warm, use a sharp knife and carefully cut the shortbread into 16 squares. Transfer to a rack to cool completely.

16 shortbread

LIME SHORTBREAD

NOTATIONS

Lime imparts a clean, citrusy flavor to these dainty, buttery cookies. They're perfect for nibbling at teatime.

1½ cups all-purpose flour
¾ cup unsalted butter, cut into small pieces
¾ cup confectioners' sugar
1½ tablespoons finely grated lime zest
1 tablespoon lime juice
¼ teaspoon salt
granulated sugar for dipping

1. Preheat the oven to 375°.

2. Put the flour, butter, sugar, lime zest, lime juice, and salt in the bowl of a food processor and pulse until the dough comes together. Remove the dough to a piece of wax paper.

3. Roll the dough into a log, 12 inches long. Slice the log into ½-inch thick rounds. Flatten each piece of dough to form a 2-inch round. Dip one side into granulated sugar.

4. Place the cookies, sugar side up on ungreased cookie sheets, 2 inches apart.

5. Bake for 10 to 12 minutes until lightly golden around the edges. Let the cookies sit on the baking sheets for 1 minute, then remove to racks to cool completely.

24 cookies

PECAN SHORTBREAD

NOTATIONS

These shortbreads are a descendant of Pecan Butterballs in my *Home Cooking*. Even though they share the same ingredients, this presentation is easier and faster, and everywhere as delicious.

1/2 cup unsalted butter, at room temperature
1/2 cup confectioners' sugar
1 tablespoon vanilla
1 cup all-purpose flour
1/4 teaspoon salt
1 cup finely ground pecans (Use a food processor.)
confectioners' sugar for sprinkling

1. Preheat the oven to 325°.

2. In a bowl with an electric mixer, cream the butter, sugar, and vanilla until fluffy. Add the flour and salt, mixing well.

3. Add the pecans and mix until evenly blended.

4. Spread the dough onto the bottom of a 9-inch springform pan. Cover the dough with a piece of plastic wrap and pat down the dough until it is even. Remove the plastic wrap. Cut the round into 8 equal wedges.

5. Bake for 30 to 35 minutes until lightly golden. While still warm, re-cut the shortbread into the wedges. Dust generously with confectioners' sugar. Remove the sides from the springform pan and transfer the shortbread to a rack to cool.

8 shortbread

CONGO BARS

NOTATIONS

The crispy exterior coupled with the chewy, chocolaty interior makes these butterscotch brownies the toast of the town. They're punctuated with chopped semi-sweet chocolate as well as semi-sweet chocolate chips. The chopped chocolate will melt somewhat during baking; the chips will retain their shape, providing a double chocolate experience.

9 tablespoons (1/2 cup plus 1 tablespoon) unsalted butter, at room temperature
1 3/4 cups light brown sugar
2 eggs
1 tablespoon vanilla
1 1/3 cups all-purpose flour
1 1/2 teaspoons baking soda
1/4 teaspoon salt
1/2 cup mini semi-sweet chocolate chips
3 ounces semi-sweet chocolate, chopped

1. Preheat the oven to 350°. Line a 9 x 13-inch pan with parchment paper, letting it overhang the pan on either end.

2. In a bowl with an electric mixer, cream the butter and sugar until fluffy. Add the eggs and vanilla and mix well.

3. Sift the flour, baking soda, and salt and add to the batter, mixing until evenly incorporated.

4. Add the chips and chopped chocolate, stirring until evenly combined. Spread the mixture into the prepared pan.

5. Bake for about 30 minutes until a toothpick inserted in the center comes out clean. Remove to a rack to cool for 1 hour; then using the parchment overhang, lift the mixture out of the pan and cut into bars.

24 bars

CRANBERRY-PECAN GRAHAMS

NOTATIONS

These graham cracker bars are chewy, fruity, and nutty. They're encrusted with pecans and dried cranberries, a most stylish combination, making these squares a number one favorite during the holiday season.

1½ cups graham cracker crumbs
½ teaspoon cinnamon
¼ teaspoon salt
½ cup dried cranberries
1 cup chopped pecans
14-ounce can sweetened condensed milk
2 tablespoons sugar

1. Preheat the oven to 350°. Line the bottom of an 8-inch square pan with parchment paper, letting it overhang the pan on two opposite sides. Grease the exposed sides of the pan.

2. In a bowl, combine the graham cracker crumbs, cinnamon, salt, cranberries, and pecans and mix well. Add the condensed milk, mixing until evenly combined.

3. Spread the mixture in the prepared pan. Sprinkle with the sugar.

4. Bake for about 35 minutes until golden and a toothpick inserted in the center comes out clean. Place on a rack to cool completely; then using the parchment overhang, lift the bars out of the pan. Cut into squares and serve.

25 squares

NOTATIONS

DATE-NUT SQUARES

Popular in the 50s, this retro bar is updated to fashionable fare. Chock full of lush dates and chunky with walnuts, they're sweet, rich, and delicious.

6 tablespoons unsalted butter, at room temperature
3/4 cup dark brown sugar
2 eggs
2 teaspoons vanilla
3/4 cup all-purpose flour
1 teaspoon baking soda
1/4 teaspoon salt
1 cup chopped pitted dates
1 cup chopped walnuts
confectioners' sugar for dusting

1. Preheat the oven to 350°. Line an 8-inch square pan with foil, letting the foil overhang the pan on two opposite sides. Grease the foil.

2. In a bowl with an electric mixer, cream the butter and sugar until fluffy. Add the eggs and vanilla and mix well.

3. Add the flour, baking soda, and salt, mixing until evenly blended. Stir in the dates and walnuts. Spread the batter in the prepared pan.

4. Bake for 25 to 30 minutes until a toothpick inserted in the center comes out clean. Place on a rack to cool completely; then using the foil overhanging, lift the bars out of the pan. Cut into squares and dust with confectioners' sugar.

16 squares

HONEY AND OATS GRANOLA

NOTATIONS

Granola is noted for its natural wholesomeness. This crunchy, healthy version is jam-packed with oats, almonds, and raisins, and perfumed with cinnamon and vanilla. Try adding this cereal-treat to yogurt, as a mix-in for ice cream, or simply for eating out of hand.

6 cups old-fashioned oats
1 1/2 cups slivered almonds
2 teaspoons cinnamon
1 cup honey
1/3 cup olive oil (not extra-virgin)
1 tablespoon vanilla
1 1/2 cups raisins

1. Preheat the oven to 350°. Grease two 9 x 13-inch baking pans.

2. In a large bowl, combine the oats, almonds, and cinnamon and mix well.

3. In a separate bowl, combine the honey, oil, and vanilla, stirring until evenly mixed.

4. Add the honey mixture to the oats, stirring until evenly moist. Divide the mixture between the two baking pans, spreading it out evenly.

5. Bake for 15 to 20 minutes until golden. Remove the pans to racks. While the granola is still warm, stir the mixture with a spatula, releasing it from the bottom and sides of the baking pans.

6. Let the granola cool completely; then stir in the raisins. Remove the granola to an airtight container.

13 1/2 cups granola

NOTATIONS

OATMEAL-RAISIN COOKIE BARS

If you're an oatmeal cookie aficionado, then you're in for a treat. Humming with old-fashioned goodness, these chewy bars are packed with cinnamon-flavored oats and are chunky with raisins. Even though these bars share very similar ingredients with the Oatmeal-Chocolate Chip Cookies in this book, the presentation gives them a different personality.

3/4 cup unsalted butter, at room temperature
3/4 cup packed dark brown sugar
1/4 cup granulated sugar
1 egg
1 teaspoon vanilla
1 cup all-purpose flour
1/4 teaspoon salt
1 teaspoon cinnamon
2 cups old-fashioned oats
3/4 cup raisins

1. Preheat the oven to 350°. Line an 8-inch square pan with parchment paper, letting it overhang the pan on two opposite sides. Grease the exposed sides of the pan.

2. In a large bowl with an electric mixer, beat the butter and sugars until fluffy. Add the egg and vanilla and mix well.

3. Add the flour, salt, and cinnamon, mixing until evenly incorporated. Mix in the oats and raisins.

4. Transfer the dough to the prepared pan. With moistened fingers, press it evenly into place to conform to the shape of the pan.

5. Bake for 30 minutes until lightly golden. Run a knife along the edges of the pan. Using the parchment overhanging, lift the bar mixture out of the pan to a rack to cool completely. Cut into squares and serve.

25 squares

CHOCOLATE CHIP-PEANUT BUTTER BARS

NOTATIONS

Packed with old-fashioned goodness—oats, peanut butter, and dark chocolate chips—these bars are always a popular choice. We never seem to tire of this theme.

1/2 cup unsalted butter, at room temperature
1/2 cup granulated sugar
1/2 cup packed light brown sugar
1 egg
1/2 cup chunky peanut butter
1 1/2 teaspoons vanilla
1 cup all-purpose flour
1/4 teaspoon salt
1/2 cup old-fashioned oats
1 cup bittersweet chocolate chips

1. Preheat the oven to 350°. Line an 8-inch square pan with foil, letting it overhang the pan on two opposite sides.

2. In a large bowl with an electric mixer, cream the butter and sugars until fluffy. Add the egg, peanut butter, and vanilla and beat until evenly mixed.

3. Mix in the flour and salt. Add the oats and chocolate chips and beat until evenly distributed. Spread the mixture in the prepared pan.

4. Bake for 20 to 25 minutes until golden brown and a toothpick inserted in the center comes out clean. Remove to a rack to cool completely. Using the foil overhang, lift the mixture out of the pan and cut into squares.

25 squares

NOTATIONS

RASPBERRY-COCONUT BARS

These bars ooze with chewy, gooey essence. The sweet, luscious raspberry layer is juxtaposed to the exotic coconut topping. They're sinfully rich and absolutely delicious!

1 cup all-purpose flour
1 teaspoon baking powder
1/4 teaspoon salt
1/2 cup cold unsalted butter, cut into small pieces
1 egg, beaten
1 tablespoon heavy cream
1/2 cup raspberry preserves
Coconut Topping (recipe follows)

1. Preheat the oven to 350°. Line an 8-inch square pan with foil, letting the foil overhang the pan on two opposite sides. Grease the foil.

2. In a bowl, combine the flour, baking powder, and salt and mix well. Using a pastry blender or fork, cut in the butter until the texture of coarse meal.

3. Add the egg and cream and mix until the dough is smooth. Transfer the dough to the prepared pan. Using moistened fingers, spread the dough out evenly to conform to the shape of the pan.

4. Spread the preserves on the crust.

5. Cover the preserve layer with the coconut topping, spreading it evenly.

6. Bake for 30 to 35 minutes until golden. Place on a rack to cool completely; then using the foil overhang, lift the mixture out of the pan and cut into squares.

Coconut Topping:
1 cup sugar
4 tablespoons unsalted butter, melted and cooled
1 egg, beaten
1 teaspoon almond extract
2 cups sweetened, shredded coconut

In a bowl, combine the sugar and butter and mix well. Stir in the egg and almond extract. Add the coconut, mixing until evenly combined.

16 squares

CHOCOLATE CHIP-COFFEE BISCOTTI

NOTATIONS

Laced with Kahlúa and studded with mini chocolate chips, these espresso-infused Italian biscuits are a coffee lovers' nirvana.

2 tablespoons Kahlúa
2 tablespoons instant espresso coffee powder
1/2 cup unsalted butter, at room temperature
1 cup sugar
2 eggs
2 cups all-purpose flour
1 1/2 teaspoons baking powder
1/4 teaspoon salt
1 cup mini semi-sweet chocolate chips

1. Preheat the oven to 325°. Line two baking sheets with parchment paper.

2. In a small bowl, combine the Kahlúa and espresso powder. Let sit for 15 minutes for the coffee to dissolve, stirring occasionally.

3. In a large bowl with an electric mixer, cream the butter and sugar. Add the eggs and Kahlua mixture, beating until evenly combined.

4. Add the flour, baking powder, and salt and mix well.

5. Stir in the chocolate chips.

6. Divide the dough in half. Turn each half out onto a baking sheet and form into a log, 3 inches wide and 12 inches long.

7. Bake for 30 minutes. Lift the parchment paper with the logs from the baking sheets to a board to cool for 5 minutes. Slice each log into 16 pieces (3/4-inch wide). Place a rack on each cookie sheet and place the slices on the racks, 1/2-inch apart.

8. Return the cookies to the oven and bake for 15 minutes more. Remove the racks from the baking sheets and let the biscotti cool completely. Store in an air-tight tin.

32 biscotti

MAGIC COOKIE BAR BISCOTTI

NOTATIONS

These biscotti are reminiscent of seven layer bars. They're plump with chocolate chips, coconut, and walnuts, making these the cookie choice du jour.

2 eggs, beaten
3/4 cup sugar
1/2 cup olive oil (not extra-virgin)
1 teaspoon vanilla
2 cups all-purpose flour
1 1/2 teaspoons baking powder
1/4 teaspoon salt
2/3 cup semi-sweet chocolate chips
2/3 cup sweetened, shredded coconut
1 cup chopped walnuts

1. Preheat the oven to 325°. Line two baking sheets with parchment paper.

2. In a large mixing bowl, combine the eggs, sugar, oil, and vanilla.

3. Add the flour, baking powder, and salt and mix well.

4. Stir in the chocolate chips, coconut, and walnuts.

5. Divide the dough in half. Turn each half out onto a baking sheet and form into a log, 3 inches wide and 13 inches long.

6. Bake for 30 minutes. Lift the parchment paper with the logs from the baking sheets to a board and let cool for 5 minutes. Slice each log into 18 pieces (3/4-inch wide). Place a rack on each cookie sheet and place the slices on the racks, 1/2-inch apart.

7. Return the cookies to the oven and bake for 15 minutes more. Remove the racks from the baking sheets and let the biscotti cool completely. Store in an air-tight tin.

3 dozen biscotti

CRANBERRY-WHITE CHOCOLATE BISCOTTI

NOTATIONS

Biscotti are the Italian-style cookies that have become the toast of the town, featured in coffee houses and pastry shops. This rendition is jam-packed with cranberries, white chocolate chips, and candied ginger. What could be better?

2 eggs, beaten
3/4 cup sugar
1/2 cup olive oil (not extra-virgin)
1 teaspoon vanilla
2 cups all-purpose flour
1 1/2 teaspoons baking powder
1/4 teaspoon salt
2 tablespoons finely chopped candied, crystallized ginger
2/3 cup dried cranberries
2/3 cup white chocolate chips

1. Preheat the oven to 325°. Line two baking sheets with parchment paper.

2. In a large bowl, combine the eggs, sugar, oil, and vanilla.

3. Add the flour, baking powder, and salt and mix well.

4. Stir in the candied ginger, cranberries, and white chocolate chips.

5. Divide the dough in half. Turn each half out onto a baking sheet and form into a log, 3 inches wide and 12 inches long.

6. Bake for 30 minutes. Lift the parchment paper with the logs from the baking sheets to a board and let cool for 5 minutes. Slice each log into 16 pieces (3/4-inch wide). Place a rack on each cookie sheet and place the slices on the racks, 1/2-inch apart.

7. Return the cookies to the oven and bake for 15 minutes more. Remove the racks from the baking sheets and let the biscotti cool completely. Store in an air-tight tin.

32 biscotti

GINGERBREAD BISCOTTI

NOTATIONS

Modeled after the ever popular gingerbread cookie, these biscotti are especially popular confections at holiday time. They're crisp, crunchy, and scented with warm spices, making them perfect for dunking into egg nog.

1/2 cup unsalted butter, at room temperature
1 cup packed dark brown sugar
2 eggs
2 cups all-purpose flour
1 teaspoon baking soda
1/4 teaspoon salt
2 teaspoons ground ginger
1 teaspoon cinnamon
1/4 teaspoon allspice
confectioners' sugar for dusting

1. Preheat the oven to 325°. Line two baking sheets with parchment paper.

2. In a large bowl with an electric mixer, cream the butter and brown sugar. Add the eggs and mix well.

3. Add the flour, baking soda, salt, and spices and mix well.

4. Divide the dough in half. Turn each half out onto a baking sheet and form into a log, 3 inches wide and 10 inches long.

5. Bake for 30 minutes. Lift the parchment paper with the logs from the baking sheets to a board and let cool for 5 minutes. Slice each log into 16 pieces (3/4-inch wide). Place a rack on each cookie sheet and place the slices on the racks, 1/2-inch apart.

6. Return the cookies to the oven and bake for 15 minutes more. Remove the racks from the baking sheets. While the biscotti are warm, dust generously with confectioners' sugar. Let cool completely. Re-dust with the sugar if necessary and store in an air-tight tin.

32 biscotti

HAZELNUT BISCOTTI

NOTATIONS

Hazelnuts are the key ingredient in these crunchy, buttery cookies. Prized for their creamy meat, delicate taste, and fragrance, they lend distinction to these Italian-style cookies.

1 cup hazelnuts
1/2 cup unsalted butter, at room temperature
3/4 cup sugar
2 eggs
2 tablespoons Frangelico (hazelnut liqueur)
2 cups all-purpose flour
1 1/2 teaspoons baking powder
1/4 teaspoon salt
confectioners' sugar for dusting

1. Preheat the oven to 400°.

2. Put the nuts in a rimmed baking pan. Toast in the oven for 5 minutes until the skins blister. Remove from the oven and let cool; then transfer the nuts to a kitchen towel and rub off as much of the skins as possible.

3. Chop the nuts.

4. Lower the oven temperature to 325°. Line two baking sheets with parchment paper.

5. In a large bowl with an electric mixer, cream the butter and sugar. Add the eggs and Frangelico and mix until evenly combined.

6. Add the flour, baking powder, and salt and mix well.

7. Stir in the hazelnuts.

8. Divide the dough in half. Turn each half out onto a baking sheet and form into a log, 3 inches wide and 12 inches long.

9. Bake for 30 minutes. Lift the parchment paper with the logs from the cookie sheets to a board and let cool for 5 minutes. Slice each log into 16 pieces (3/4-inch wide). Place a rack on each cookie sheet and place the slices on the racks, 1/2-inch apart.

10. Return the cookies to the oven and bake for 15 minutes more. Remove the racks from the baking sheets and let the biscotti cool completely. Dust with confectioners' sugar and serve. Store in an airtight tin.

32 biscotti

PISTACHIO BISCOTTI

NOTATIONS

These almond-scented biscotti are studded with pistachio nuts. These mild-flavored green jewels have become a popular favorite for munching—they're not only delicious, they're also nutritious. No one can eat just one!

1/2 cup unsalted butter, at room temperature
1 cup sugar
2 eggs
2 tablespoons Amaretto
2 cups all-purpose flour
1 1/2 teaspoons baking powder
1/4 teaspoon salt
1 cup shelled pistachio nuts, chopped

1. Preheat the oven to 325°. Line two baking sheets with parchment paper.

2. In a large bowl with an electric mixer, cream the butter and sugar. Add the eggs and Amaretto and mix until evenly combined.

3. Add the flour, baking powder, and salt and mix well.

4. Stir in the pistachio nuts.

5. Divide the dough in half. Turn each half out onto a baking sheet and form into a log, 3 inches wide and 12 inches long.

6. Bake for 30 minutes. Lift the parchment paper with the logs from the cookie sheets to a board and let cool for 5 minutes. Slice each log into 16 pieces (3/4-inch wide). Place a rack on each cookie sheet and place the slices on the racks, 1/2-inch apart.

7. Return the cookies to the oven for 15 minutes more. Remove the racks from the baking sheets and let the biscotti cool completely. Store in an air-tight tin.

32 biscotti

CAKES, PIES, AND PASTRIES

BANANA CAKE

NOTATIONS

This perfectly moist, cinnamon-infused, banana-rich cake gets a thumbs up. It's frosted with a sweet vanilla butter cream that definitely steps up the infamous homespun banana bread. (The riper the bananas are, the sweeter the cake will be.)

1/2 cup unsalted butter, at room temperature
1 cup sugar
2 eggs
1 1/2 teaspoons vanilla
2 large, ripe bananas, peeled and mashed
3/4 cup sour cream
2 cups all-purpose flour
1 teaspoon baking powder
1 teaspoon baking soda
1/4 teaspoon salt
Vanilla Butter Cream (recipe follows)

1. Preheat the oven to 350°. Grease a 9-inch square pan.

2. In a large bowl with an electric mixer, cream the butter and sugar until fluffy. Add the eggs and vanilla and mix well.

3. Mix in the bananas and sour cream.

4. Sift together the flour, baking powder, baking soda, and salt and add these to the batter, mixing until evenly combined. Transfer the batter to the prepared pan.

5. Bake for about 35 minutes until a toothpick inserted in the center comes out clean. Place on a rack to cool completely. Frost with the vanilla butter cream and serve.

9 or more portions

Vanilla Butter Cream:
1 1/2 cups confectioners' sugar
4 tablespoons unsalted butter, at room temperature
1/2 teaspoon vanilla
1 tablespoon heavy cream

In a bowl with an electric mixer, cream the sugar and butter until fluffy. Add the vanilla and cream and beat until smooth. Refrigerate until needed.

BROWN SUGAR-STREUSEL CRUMB CAKE

NOTATIONS

This fluffy, light-textured coffee cake is scented with cinnamon and sports a yummy, buttery, brown sugar-streusel topping. This little slice of comfort is great for Sunday brunch with mugs of coffee.

2 cups all-purpose flour
1 teaspoon cinnamon
1 3/8 cups lightly packed dark brown sugar
10 tablespoons cold unsalted butter, cut into small pieces
1 1/2 teaspoons baking powder
1/2 teaspoon baking soda
1/4 teaspoon salt
2 eggs, beaten
2 teaspoons vanilla
1 cup whole milk

1. Preheat the oven to 375°. Grease a 9-inch square baking pan.

2. In a large bowl, whisk together the flour and cinnamon. Mix in the brown sugar.

3. Using a pastry blender or fork, cut the butter into the flour mixture until the texture of coarse meal. Remove 1 cup of the streusel and set aside.

4. Add the baking powder, baking soda, and salt to the flour mixture, stirring until evenly combined.

5. In a separate small bowl, combine the eggs, vanilla, and milk. Add to the dry ingredients, mixing only until smooth.

6. Turn the batter into the prepared pan.

7. Sprinkle the reserved crumb mixture evenly over the batter.

8. Bake for 30 minutes until a toothpick inserted in the center comes out clean. Transfer the pan to a rack to cool completely.

9 portions

NOTATIONS

CHERRY YOGURT CAKE

This homespun fruit cake is resplendent with plump, sweet cherries. Thick, lush Greek yogurt helps to make the cake fluffy, moist, and light textured. You don't have to be a yogurt fan to enjoy this dessert.

1/4 cup unsalted butter, at room temperature
2/3 cup plus 2 tablespoons sugar
1 egg
1 teaspoon vanilla
1 cup all-purpose flour
1/2 teaspoon baking powder
1/2 teaspoon baking soda
1/4 teaspoon salt
1/2 cup whole milk Greek yogurt
1 cup pitted cherries, halved and dusted with 1 tablespoon flour

1. Preheat the oven to 400°. Grease a 9-inch round layer cake pan.

2. In a bowl with an electric mixer, cream the butter and 2/3 cup sugar until fluffy. Add the egg and vanilla and mix well.

3. Sift together the flour, baking powder, baking soda, and salt. Add the dry ingredients alternately with the yogurt to the batter, mixing until evenly incorporated.

4. Stir in the cherries. Turn the batter into the prepared pan, spreading it evenly. Sprinkle the top with the 2 tablespoons sugar.

5. Bake for 25 to 30 minutes until a toothpick inserted in the center comes out clean. Place on a rack to cool for 5 minutes; then run a knife around the edge of the cake and remove the cake from the pan. Serve warm or let cool on a rack and serve at room temperature.

6 portions

SPICED CORNBREAD

NOTATIONS

This sweet version of the all-American favorite is scented with cinnamon, ginger, and allspice, elevating the already delicious classic to gastronomic heights. It's perfect for breakfast, brunch, and teatime.

1 1/4 cups all-purpose flour
3/4 cup cornmeal
3/4 cup sugar
2 teaspoons baking powder
1/2 teaspoon baking soda
1/2 teaspoon salt
1 teaspoon cinnamon
1/4 teaspoon ground ginger
1/4 teaspoon allspice
1/2 cup unsalted butter, melted and cooled
2 eggs, beaten
1 cup buttermilk
1 tablespoon vanilla

1. Preheat the oven to 375°. Grease an 8-inch square pan.

2. In a large mixing bowl, combine the flour, cornmeal, sugar, baking powder, baking soda, salt, and spices and mix well.

3. In a separate small bowl, whisk together the butter, eggs, buttermilk, and vanilla.

4. Add the wet ingredients to the flour mixture, stirring gently only until evenly combined. Turn the batter into the prepared pan.

5. Bake for 30 to 35 minutes until a toothpick inserted in the center comes out clean. Serve warm or at room temperature. I like to garnish the cake with whipped cream and berries.

9 portions

CINNAMON-MAPLE CAKE

NOTATIONS

This delicate, brown sugar cake is infused with maple syrup and flavored with cinnamon. The maple syrup lends a slightly smoky flavor to the batter. For a grand finale, it's crowned with a cloud of cinnamon-scented whipped cream, making it an elegant ending to any meal.

1/2 cup unsalted butter, at room temperature
1/2 cup firmly packed light brown sugar
2 eggs
6 tablespoons pure maple syrup
1 1/2 cups all-purpose flour
1 teaspoon baking soda
1/2 teaspoon salt
1 teaspoon cinnamon
2/3 cup buttermilk
Cinnamon Whipped Cream (recipe follows)

1. Preheat the oven to 325°. Grease an 8-inch square pan.

2. In a large bowl with an electric mixer, cream the butter and sugar until fluffy. Add the eggs and maple syrup and mix well.

3. Sift together the flour, baking soda, salt, and cinnamon. Add the dry ingredients alternately with the buttermilk to the batter, mixing until evenly incorporated. Turn the batter into the prepared pan.

4. Bake for 40 to 45 minutes until a toothpick inserted in the center comes out clean. Place on a rack to cool completely.

5. Cut into individual portions and serve with dollops of cinnamon whipped cream.

8 portions

Cinnamon Whipped Cream:
1 cup heavy cream
1/4 cup confectioners' sugar
1 teaspoon cinnamon

In a bowl with an electric mixer, whip the cream, sugar, and cinnamon until stiff peaks form. Refrigerate until needed.

GINGER CREAM CAKE

This light-textured, coffee-infused cake boasts a lush ginger scent and flavor. It's absolutely heavenly and is particularly delicious when topped with coffee ice cream.

NOTATIONS

1 cup heavy cream
1 tablespoon instant coffee powder
1 1/2 cups sugar
4 eggs
1 3/4 cups all-purpose flour
1 1/2 teaspoons baking powder
1/2 teaspoon baking soda
1/4 teaspoon salt
1 1/2 teaspoons ground ginger
2 tablespoons minced candied, crystallized ginger
confectioners' sugar for dusting

1. In a small bowl, combine the heavy cream and coffee powder. Let sit for 15 minutes for the coffee to dissolve completely, stirring occasionally.

2. Preheat the oven to 400°. Grease and flour a 10-inch tube pan.

3. In a large bowl with an electric mixer, beat the sugar and eggs until thick and pale lemon colored.

4. Sift together the flour, baking powder, baking soda, salt, and ginger. Add the dry ingredients alternately with the coffee cream to the batter. Mix in the candied ginger. Turn the batter into the prepared pan.

5. Bake for 15 minutes. Reduce the oven temperature to 300° and bake for 30 minutes more. Remove to a rack to cool for 10 minutes. Remove the tube from the pan to the rack and let the cake cool completely.

6. Run a knife under the bottom of the cake to release it from the pan. Invert the cake onto a plate, then using a second plate, turn the cake right side up. Dust with confectioners' sugar and serve.

8 to 10 portions

RICOTTA-FIG CAKE

NOTATIONS

This superbly moist and fruity cake is distinguished by dried figs and orange zest. The figs add a sweet, rich flavor, giving rise to an elegant, year-round finale whether served unadorned or with dollops of whipped cream.

1 cup dried figs, stems removed
1 tablespoon all-purpose flour
1/2 cup unsalted butter, at room temperature
1 1/4 cups sugar
2 eggs
1 cup whole milk ricotta cheese
1 tablespoon grated orange zest
2 cups all-purpose flour
1 teaspoon baking powder
1 teaspoon baking soda
1/2 teaspoon salt
1/2 cup whole milk
1/4 cup orange juice
confectioners' sugar for dusting

1. Preheat the oven to 350°. Grease a 10-inch tube pan.

2. Chop the figs into 1/4-inch cubes. Dust with 1 tablespoon flour.

3. In a large bowl with an electric mixer, cream the butter and sugar until fluffy. Add the eggs, ricotta, and orange zest and mix well.

4. Sift together the flour, baking powder, baking soda, and salt. Combine the milk and orange juice. Add the dry ingredients alternately with the milk mixture to the batter, beating until evenly incorporated.

5. Mix in the dried figs. Turn the batter into the prepared pan.

6. Bake for 40 minutes until a toothpick inserted in the center comes out clean. Remove the tube from the pan, place on a rack, and let the cake cool completely.

7. Run a knife under the bottom of the cake to release it from the pan. Invert the cake onto a plate, then using a second plate, turn the cake right side up. Dust with confectioners' sugar and serve.

10 to 12 servings

CRANBERRY-NUT UPSIDE-DOWN CAKE

NOTATIONS

Pineapple is customarily the fruit of choice in an upside-down cake. I've expanded on the theme and have featured cranberries and walnuts. An upside-down cake is unique—once baked, the cake is inverted and the fruity-nut base forms a cloying, syrupy topping for the cake. It definitely has the wow factor.

Topping:
4 tablespoons unsalted butter, melted
3/4 cup packed dark brown sugar
1 1/3 cups cranberries
2/3 cup chopped walnuts

Cake:
1/2 cup unsalted butter, at room temperature
1 cup granulated sugar
2 eggs
1 teaspoon vanilla
1 1/2 teaspoons grated orange zest
1 3/4 cups all-purpose flour
1 1/2 teaspoons baking powder
1/2 teaspoon salt
1 teaspoon cinnamon
2/3 cup buttermilk

1. Preheat the oven to 350°. Grease the bottom and sides of a 9-inch round cake pan. Line the bottom with parchment paper and grease the paper.

2. Prepare the topping. In a bowl, combine the butter and sugar, stirring until evenly combined. Add the cranberries and nuts and mix well. Spread the mixture evenly in the prepared pan.

3. Prepare the cake. In a large bowl with an electric mixer, cream the butter and sugar until fluffy. Add the eggs, vanilla, and orange zest and mix well.

4. Sift together the flour, baking powder, salt, and cinnamon. Add the dry ingredients alternately with the buttermilk to the batter, mixing until combined. Spread the batter evenly over the cranberry-nut mixture.

NOTATIONS

5. Bake for 45 to 50 minutes until a toothpick inserted in the center comes out clean. Remove to a rack to cool for 15 minutes; then run a knife around the edge of the pan. Invert the cake onto a large plate. Lift off the pan. Peel off the parchment paper, scraping any residual topping onto bald spots of the cake. Serve warm or at room temperature.

8 to 10 portions

CRUMB CAKE REVISISTED

NOTATIONS

I've put a spin on this family favorite, making it even better. It made its debut in my ***Uncommon Gourmet Cookbook***. This light-textured cake is distinctly vanilla-scented and encrusted with a yummy, buttery crumb topping.

6 tablespoons cold unsalted butter, cut into small pieces
1 1/2 cups sugar
1 3/4 cups all-purpose flour
2 teaspoons baking powder
1/2 teaspoon salt
2 eggs, separated
3/4 cup buttermilk
1 tablespoon vanilla

1. Preheat the oven to 350°. Grease a 10-inch tube pan.

2. In a large bowl with an electric mixer, cream the butter and sugar until the texture of cornmeal.

3. Sift together the flour, baking powder, and salt. Add the dry ingredients to the sugar mixture, beating only until crumbly. Remove a heaping 1/2 cup of the mixture and reserve it for the topping.

4. Add the egg yolks, buttermilk, and vanilla to the bowl, mixing gently until smooth.

5. In a separate bowl, beat the egg whites until stiff. Using a spatula, gently fold them into the cake batter until no traces of white remain.

6. Pour the batter into the prepared pan. Sprinkle the reserved crumb mixture evenly over the top of the cake.

7. Bake for 40 minutes or until a cake tester inserted in the middle of the cake comes out clean. Remove to a rack to cool for 30 minutes; then remove the tube from the pan and let the cake cool completely. When ready to serve, run a knife under the bottom of the cake to release it from the pan. Invert the cake onto a plate, then using a second plate, turn the cake right side up, and present.

8 portions

NOTATIONS

MARBLE CAKE

Can't decide if you want vanilla or chocolate cake? Don't fret—this cake offers both. The moist vanilla-based cake is rippled with a semi-sweet chocolate swirl for total satisfaction.

3 ounces semi-sweet chocolate, chopped
1 cup sugar
3 eggs
1/2 cup unsalted butter, melted and cooled
1 1/2 teaspoons vanilla
1 1/2 cups all-purpose flour
3/4 teaspoon baking powder
1/4 teaspoon salt
1/2 cup sour cream
1 pint vanilla ice cream, thawed to the consistency of sour cream

1. Preheat the oven to 375°. Grease and flour a 9-inch round cake pan.

2. In the top of a double boiler over simmering water, heat the chocolate, stirring until melted and smooth. Remove from the heat and let cool.

3. In a large bowl with an electric mixer, beat the sugar and eggs until pale lemon colored. Add the butter and vanilla and mix well.

4. Sift together the flour, baking powder, and salt. Add the dry ingredients alternately with the sour cream to the batter, mixing until evenly incorporated.

5. Pour 2/3 of the batter into the prepared pan. Add the cooled chocolate to the remaining batter, mixing until evenly blended.

6. Spoon dollops of the chocolate batter over the vanilla batter in the pan. Using a spatula or knife, ripple the batter, creating a marbling effect.

7. Bake for 30 to 35 minutes until a toothpick inserted in the center of the cake comes out slightly moist. The top of the cake will be slightly mounded and cracked—as the cake cools, the cracks will come together slightly. Place on a rack to cool completely.

8. To serve, ladle spoonfuls of the softened vanilla ice cream onto each plate. Place a slice of cake on top of the luscious vanilla sauce and present.

6 to 8 portions

FROSTED GINGERBREAD

I've put a new twist on good old-fashioned gingerbread from my ***All-Occasion Cookbook***. Warm with aromatic spices and infused with the smokiness of molasses, this updated cake is also studded with raisins and candied ginger. The crowning glory is its vanilla butter cream that separates this gingerbread from all others.

NOTATIONS

1/2 cup unsalted butter, at room temperature
1/2 cup packed light brown sugar
1 egg
2/3 cup unsulfured molasses
1 3/4 cups all-purpose flour
1 teaspoon baking soda
1/4 teaspoon salt
1 1/2 teaspoons ground ginger
1 teaspoon cinnamon
3/4 cup buttermilk
2 tablespoons minced candied, crystallized ginger
2/3 cup raisins
Vanilla Butter Cream (recipe follows)

1. Preheat the oven to 350°. Grease a 9-inch square pan.

2. In a large bowl with an electric mixer, cream the butter and sugar until fluffy. Add the egg and molasses and mix well.

3. Sift together the flour, baking soda, salt, ginger, and cinnamon. Add the dry ingredients alternately with the buttermilk to the batter, mixing until evenly incorporated.

4. Mix in the candied ginger and raisins. Turn the batter into the prepared pan.

5. Bake for 30 to 35 minutes until the edges have pulled away from the sides of the pan and the top springs back when lightly touched. Place on a rack to cool completely. Frost with the vanilla butter cream and serve.

9 portions

NOTATIONS

Vanilla Butter Cream:
1 1/4 cups confectioners' sugar
4 tablespoons unsalted butter, at room temperature
1/2 teaspoon vanilla
1 tablespoon heavy cream

In a bowl with an electric mixer, cream the sugar and butter until fluffy. Add the vanilla and cream and beat until smooth. Refrigerate until needed.

PUMPKIN CAKE WITH MAPLE FROSTING

NOTATIONS

I've locked in the flavor of this harvest cake by adding warm spices—cinnamon, ginger, and allspice—to the pumpkin batter. The simple dessert is made magical thanks to the buttery maple-cream cheese frosting.

1/2 cup unsalted butter, melted and cooled
1 cup sugar
2 eggs
1/4 cup unsulfured molasses
15-ounce can pumpkin purée
2 cups all-purpose flour
1 teaspoon baking powder
1/2 teaspoon baking soda
1/2 teaspoon salt
1 1/2 teaspoons cinnamon
1 teaspoon ground ginger
1/2 teaspoon allspice
Maple-Cream Cheese Frosting (recipe follows)

1. Preheat the oven to 350°. Grease a 9-inch square pan.

2. In a large bowl with an electric mixer, beat the butter, sugar, eggs, and molasses until fluffy. Add the pumpkin purée and mix until evenly combined.

3. Sift together the flour, baking powder, baking soda, salt, and spices. Add to the batter, mixing until evenly incorporated. Turn the batter into the prepared pan.

4. Bake for 45 to 50 minutes until a toothpick inserted in the center comes out clean. Place on a rack to cool completely. Spread with the maple-cream cheese frosting and serve.

9 portions

Maple-Cream Cheese Frosting:
1/2 cup unsalted butter, at room temperature
1/2 pound cream cheese, at room temperature
1/4 cup pure maple syrup

In a bowl with an electric mixer, whip the butter, cream cheese, and maple syrup until evenly blended and fluffy.

LEMON CREAM CAKE

NOTATIONS

This light, ethereal cake is exquisite. It's scented with lemon essence, drizzled with a lemon icing, and crowned with coconut, making it the perfect all-occasion cake.

1½ cups sugar
4 eggs
2 tablespoons finely grated lemon zest
1 tablespoon lemon juice
1¾ cups all-purpose flour
2 teaspoons baking powder
¼ teaspoon salt
1 cup heavy cream
Lemon Glaze (recipe follows)
½ cup sweetened, shredded coconut

1. Preheat the oven to 400°. Grease and flour a 10-inch tube pan.

2. In a large bowl with an electric mixer, beat the sugar and eggs until thick and pale lemon colored. Add the lemon zest and lemon juice and mix well.

3. Sift together the flour, baking powder, and salt. Add the dry ingredients alternately with the cream to the batter, mixing gently. Turn the batter into the prepared pan.

4. Bake for 15 minutes. Reduce the oven temperature to 300° and bake for 30 minutes more until a toothpick inserted in the center comes out clean. Remove to a rack to cool for 10 minutes. Remove the tube from the pan and let the cake cool completely.

5. Run a knife under the bottom of the cake to release it from the pan. Invert the cake onto a plate, then using a second plate, turn the cake right side up. Drizzle the glaze over the top and sides of the cake; then sprinkle the top with the coconut, patting it into place. Let the glaze set for 2 hours before serving.

8 to 10 portions

Lemon Glaze:
1¼ cups confectioners' sugar
2 tablespoons lemon juice

In a bowl, mix the sugar and lemon juice until smooth.

GINGERBREAD PUDDING CAKE

NOTATIONS

This cake is most unusual. As it bakes, the bottom becomes a velvety butterscotch pudding, while the top turns into a light, spiced gingerbread. The creamy pudding is served as a sauce atop the ginger cake, making this a lip-smacking experience.

Cake:
1 cup all-purpose flour
1/3 cup sugar
3/4 teaspoon baking soda
1/4 teaspoon salt
1 teaspoon ground ginger
1 teaspoon cinnamon
1/4 teaspoon ground cloves
1/4 cup molasses
1/4 cup whole milk
4 tablespoons unsalted butter, melted

Pudding:
3/4 cup packed light brown sugar
1 1/2 cups boiling water

1. Preheat the oven to 350°.

2. In a large bowl, combine the flour, sugar, baking soda, salt, ginger, cinnamon, and cloves and mix well.

3. Add the molasses, milk, and melted butter and stir until evenly mixed. Transfer the batter to an ungreased 8-inch square pan.

4. Make the pudding. In a small bowl, combine the brown sugar and boiling water, stirring until the sugar is dissolved. Pour this mixture over the cake batter—do not stir.

5. Bake for 30 to 35 minutes until the top is set. Serve warm with the pudding spooned over the cake. I like to serve a scoop of vanilla ice cream alongside.

6 to 8 portions

NOTATIONS

YELLOW CAKE WITH CHOCOLATE FROSTING

This old-time favorite is a sure crowd pleaser. This no frills dessert showcases a yellow sheet cake that's buried under a cloying, chocolate butter cream frosting.

2 cups sugar
4 eggs
1 tablespoon vanilla
1/2 cup olive oil (not extra-virgin)
3 cups all-purpose flour
1 tablespoon baking powder
1/4 teaspoon salt
1 cup light cream
Chocolate Frosting (recipe follows)

1. Preheat the oven to 325°. Grease a 9 x 13-inch baking pan.

2. In a large bowl with an electric mixer, beat the sugar and eggs until fluffy. Add the vanilla and oil and mix well.

3. Sift together the flour, baking powder, and salt. Add the dry ingredients alternately with the cream to the batter, mixing until evenly incorporated. Turn the batter into the prepared pan.

4. Bake for 30 to 35 minutes until a toothpick inserted in the center comes out clean. Place on a rack to cool completely. Spread with the chocolate frosting and serve.

16 portions

Chocolate Frosting:
4 cups confectioners' sugar
1/2 cup unsalted butter, at room temperature
1 1/2 teaspoons vanilla
1/2 cup unsweetened cocoa
5 tablespoons light cream

In a bowl with an electric mixer, cream the sugar and butter until fluffy. Add the vanilla, cocoa, and cream and beat until smooth. Refrigerate until needed.

STRAWBERRIES AND CREAM BABY CAKES

NOTATIONS

Strawberries and cream are a Wimbledon classic. Expanding on this winsome pairing, I've created individual frosted strawberry cakes. These jumbo-sized, moist, fruity cupcakes are glazed in a vanilla icing, making them the toast of the town.

1/2 cup unsalted butter, at room temperature
2/3 cup sugar
2 eggs
2 teaspoons vanilla
1 1/2 cups all-purpose flour
1 1/2 teaspoons baking powder
1/2 teaspoon baking soda
1/4 teaspoon salt
2/3 cup light cream
1 1/3 cups halved strawberries (quarter large strawberries), dusted with 1 tablespoon flour
3 halved strawberries for garnish
Vanilla Icing (recipe follows)

1. Preheat the oven to 375°. Grease a jumbo-size, 6-muffin pan, even if it's non-stick.

2. In a bowl with an electric mixer, cream the butter and sugar until fluffy. Add the eggs and vanilla and mix well.

3. Sift together the flour, baking powder, baking soda, and salt. Add the dry ingredients alternately with the cream to the batter, mixing until smooth.

4. Fold in the berries. Divide the batter evenly among the 6 muffin cups.

5. Bake for 20 minutes until a toothpick inserted in the center comes out clean. Place on a rack to cool for 20 to 30 minutes; then remove the muffins from the pan to the rack to cool completely. When cooled, turn the cakes upside down. Pour large spoonfuls of the icing over each baby cake, letting it drip down the sides. Garnish the top of each cake with half a strawberry. Let the icing set for 1 hour and serve. (These are best eaten the same day they're made.)

6 baby cakes

NOTATIONS

Vanilla Icing:
3 tablespoons unsalted butter, melted
$1^1/_2$ cups confectioners' sugar
1 teaspoon vanilla
2 tablespoons whole milk

In a bowl, mix the butter, sugar, vanilla, and milk until smooth.

PUMPKIN CAKE ROLL

This light-textured pumpkin cake roll is a holiday favorite. Spiced with cinnamon and nutmeg and filled with a lush ginger whipped cream, this comforting dessert is sure to make you smile.

NOTATIONS

1 cup sugar
4 eggs
2/3 cup canned pumpkin
3/4 cup all-purpose flour
1 teaspoon baking powder
1/4 teaspoon salt
1 1/2 teaspoons cinnamon
1/2 teaspoon nutmeg
pinch of ground cloves
confectioners' sugar
Ginger Cream (recipe follows)

1. Preheat the oven to 375°. Grease a 10 x 15-inch jelly-roll pan. Line the pan with parchment paper and grease the paper.

2. In a large bowl with an electric mixer, beat the sugar and eggs until pale lemon colored. Mix in the pumpkin.

3. Sift together the flour, baking powder, salt, cinnamon, nutmeg, and cloves and gently fold the dry ingredients into the batter. Pour the batter into the prepared pan and spread it evenly.

4. Bake for 15 minutes until the top springs back when gently touched. Turn the cake over onto a towel that's been dusted with confectioners' sugar. Lift off the pan and peel off the parchment paper. Carefully roll the cake lengthwise with the towel, jelly roll fashion. Let the cake remain in this position on a rack until it cools completely.

5. When the cake is cooled, unroll and fill, spreading the ginger cream evenly on the cake to within 1-inch of all edges. Carefully reroll the cake to form a log and place seam side down on a platter. Dust with confectioners' sugar and store in the refrigerator. Remove from the refrigerator 30 minutes before serving.

10 to 12 portions

NOTATIONS

Ginger Cream:
1 cup heavy cream
1/4 cup confectioners' sugar
1 teaspoon ground ginger

In a bowl with an electric mixer, whip the cream, sugar, and ginger until stiff peaks form. Refrigerate until needed.

VANILLA CUPCAKES WITH COFFEE FROSTING

NOTATIONS

Cupcakes in all their forms are the rage—everyone is enamored with the darling individual cakes. These vanilla baby cakes are crowned with an espresso-rich frosting, taking them to a whole new level of indulgence.

1/2 cup unsalted butter, at room temperature
3/4 cup sugar
2 eggs
1 tablespoon vanilla
1 1/2 cups self-rising flour
1/2 cup whole milk
Coffee Frosting (recipe follows)

1. Preheat the oven to 350°. Line a muffin pan with paper liners.

2. In a bowl with an electric mixer, cream the butter and sugar until fluffy. Add the eggs and vanilla and mix well.

3. Add the flour alternately with the milk to the batter, mixing until smooth.

4. Spoon the batter into the muffin cups, filling them 3/4 full.

5. Bake for 20 minutes until a toothpick inserted in the center comes out clean. Remove the cupcakes from the pan to a rack to cool completely. Spread the coffee frosting over the tops of the cupcakes and serve.

11 cupcakes

Coffee Frosting:
3/4 cup confectioners' sugar
4 tablespoons unsalted butter, at room temperature
1 tablespoon instant espresso coffee powder
1 1/2 teaspoons whole milk

In a bowl with an electric mixer, beat the sugar, butter, coffee powder, and milk until smooth and creamy.

NOTATIONS

DEEP-DISH CRANBERRY-NUT PIE

This easy to prepare, bottomless, fruit and nut pie is a family tradition at our Thanksgiving. Teeming with cranberries and pecans that are canopied under a golden, buttery pastry, it's the perfect balance of sweet and tart.

3 cups cranberries
2/3 cup chopped pecans
2/3 cup dark brown sugar

1. Preheat the oven to 350°. Grease a 9-inch deep-dish pie pan.

2. In a large bowl, combine the cranberries, pecans, and brown sugar. Spread the mixture in the prepared pan. Prepare the topping.

Topping:
1/2 cup unsalted butter, melted and cooled
1 cup sugar
1 egg, beaten
1 teaspoon vanilla
1/2 teaspoon cinnamon
1 cup all-purpose flour

1. In a medium-size bowl, combine the butter and sugar and mix well. Add the egg, vanilla, and cinnamon and stir until evenly combined.

2. Add the flour and mix until incorporated. Spread the batter evenly over the cranberry-nut mixture.

3. Bake for 45 minutes until golden and bubbly. Serve hot, warm, or at room temperature. My preference is warm with scoops of vanilla ice cream.

6 to 8 portions

CHOCOLATE-PEANUT BUTTER TARTLETS

NOTATIONS

Two adored classics come together in these precious little tartlets. Reese's fans will be hard-pressed to find a better version of the chocolate-peanut butter theme. I'm particularly fond of the sweet chocolate coupled with the salty peanut topping.

Crust:
1/2 cup unsalted butter, at room temperature
3 ounces cream cheese, at room temperature
1 cup all-purpose flour
pinch of salt

1. In a bowl with an electric mixer, cream the butter and cream cheese until smooth. Add the flour and salt and mix until the dough comes together. Roll the dough into a log, 12 inches. Chill the dough for 2 hours and as much as overnight.

2. Preheat the oven to 350°. Grease two mini-muffin pans.

3. Remove the dough from the refrigerator and cut the log into 24 pieces (1/2-inch wide chunks). Roll each piece into a ball and using the palm of your hand, flatten into a 2-inch round. Press each round into a cup of the muffin pans. Prick the bottom and sides of the dough with a fork.

4. Bake for 15 minutes until lightly golden. Remove the tart shells from the pans to a rack to cool completely before filling. (These may be made up to 2 weeks in advance and frozen.)

Filling:
1/4 cup creamy peanut butter
1/4 cup mascarpone cheese
1 1/2 tablespoons light brown sugar

1. In a bowl, cream the peanut butter, cheese, and sugar until evenly mixed and smooth.

2. Use 1 teaspoon of the peanut butter mixture to fill each tart shell. Prepare the topping.

NOTATIONS

Topping:
3/8 cup semi-sweet chocolate chips
1/4 cup finely chopped salted peanuts

1. In the top of a double boiler over simmering water, melt the chocolate, stirring until smooth. Remove from the heat.

2. Spread a spoonful of the melted chocolate over the peanut butter filling; then dip the chocolate into the chopped nuts, coating completely. Refrigerate for 1 hour to set the chocolate.

3. Remove from the refrigerator and let come to room temperature before serving. Store any extra in the refrigerator.

2 dozen tartlets

LEMON TARTLETS

These dainty, pop-in-the-mouth tartlets are like mini lemon meringue pies, only better. The buttery pastry shells are filled with a refreshing lemon curd, topped with crème fraîche, and crowned with fresh raspberries. They're creamy, lemony, and luscious.

NOTATIONS

Lemon Curd:
3 egg yolks (from extra-large eggs)
1/2 cup sugar
4 tablespoons unsalted butter, melted and cooled
1 tablespoon finely grated lemon zest
1/4 cup lemon juice

Put the egg yolks, sugar, butter, lemon zest, and lemon juice in a medium-size saucepan. Cook over medium-low heat, stirring occasionally, until the mixture thickens, about 10 to 12 minutes. Do not let the mixture boil. Let cool completely before using. Note—the curd will thicken more as it cools. Store in the refrigerator until needed. It will keep for 3 weeks.

about 7/8 cup lemon curd

Tart Shells:
1 cup all-purpose flour
1/2 cup cold unsalted butter, cut into small pieces
3 ounces cream cheese, at room temperature

Garnish:
crème fraîche
1 pint raspberries

1. Put the flour, butter, and cream cheese in the bowl of a food processor. Pulse until the dough comes together and forms a ball. Remove the dough to a board and roll into a log, 12 inches long. Chill the dough for 2 hours and as much as overnight.

2. Preheat the oven to 350°. Either grease two mini-muffin pans or use non-stick pans.

3. Remove the dough from the refrigerator and cut the log into 24 pieces (1/2-inch wide chunks). Roll each piece into a ball and using the palm of your hand, flatten into a 2-inch round. Press each round into a cup of the muffin pans. Prick the sides and bottom of the dough with a fork.

NOTATIONS

4. Bake for 15 minutes until golden. Remove the tart shells from the pans and place on a rack to cool completely. (These may be made up to 2 weeks in advance and frozen.)

5. When ready to serve, fill each pastry shell with 1/2 tablespoon of lemon curd, top with a dollop of crème fraîche, and garnish with a raspberry. (Do not fill the tartlets in advance as the shells will get too wet from the lemon curd.)

2 dozen tartlets

FIG TARTLETS

NOTATIONS

A buttery, cream cheese pastry forms the base for these sweet, fig-filled, pistachio-dusted tartlets. Perfectly balanced in flavor, these small bites are hard to resist.

Crust:
1/2 cup unsalted butter, at room temperature
3 ounces cream cheese, at room temperature
1 teaspoon vanilla
1 cup all-purpose flour
1/4 teaspoon salt

1. In a bowl with an electric mixer, cream the butter, cream cheese, and vanilla until smooth. Add the flour and salt and beat until evenly combined.

2. Roll the dough into a log, 12 inches long and refrigerate for 1 hour and as much as overnight.

3. Preheat the oven to 350°. Grease two mini-muffin pans.

4. Remove the dough from the refrigerator and cut the log into 24 pieces (1/2-inch wide chunks). Roll each piece into a ball and using the palm of your hand, flatten into a 2-inch round. Press each round into a cup of the muffin pans. Prick the bottom and sides of the dough with a fork.

5. Bake for 15 minutes until lightly golden. Remove the tart shells from the pans to a rack to cool completely before filling. (These can be made up to 2 weeks in advance and frozen.)

Filling:
1/2 cup fig jam or preserves
3 tablespoons finely chopped pistachio nuts

Fill each tart shell with 1 teaspoon of fig jam. Sprinkle with pistachio nuts and serve.

2 dozen tartlets

ORANGE SCONES

NOTATIONS

The hallmark of a great scone is its buttery taste and crumbly texture. This orange-scented version is a most glorious rendition. It's perfect for teatime and ever so good for breakfast with jam.

2 cups all-purpose flour
1 tablespoon baking powder
1/2 teaspoon salt
1/2 cup sugar
1 tablespoon grated orange zest
1/2 cup cold, unsalted butter, cut into small pieces
2/3 cup heavy cream
1 1/2 tablespoons sugar for sprinkling

1. Preheat the oven to 425°.

2. In a large bowl, combine the flour, baking powder, salt, sugar, and orange zest and mix well.

3. Using a pastry blender or fork, cut in the butter until the texture of coarse meal. Add the cream and mix until the dough is evenly moist.

4. Turn the dough out onto a lightly floured board and knead gently until smooth. Shape the dough into a 3/4-inch thick round. Cut into 8 wedges and sprinkle generously with the 1 1/2 tablespoons sugar. Place on an ungreased baking sheet, 2 inches apart.

5. Bake in the upper half of the oven for 13 to 15 minutes until golden and springy to the touch. Remove to a rack to cool slightly. Serve warm or at room temperature.

8 scones

MIXED BERRY SHORTCAKES

These shortcakes deviate from the classic. I've turned up the volume with a buttery, flaky scone base that's lavished with a sumptuous mascarpone cream and a trio of berries. It's sheer heaven!

NOTATIONS

Fruit Topping:
2 cups halved strawberries
1 cup raspberries
1 cup blueberries
1/4 cup raspberry preserves, melted

Put the berries in a large bowl. Add the preserves and mix gently until evenly coated. Let sit for 2 to 3 hours, allowing a sauce to form.

Mascarpone Cream:
6 ounces mascarpone cheese
3 tablespoons confectioners' sugar
3/4 teaspoon vanilla
1/4 cup sweetened, shredded coconut

In a bowl with an electric mixer, cream the cheese, sugar, and vanilla until smooth. Add the coconut and mix until evenly combined. Refrigerate until needed.

Scones:
2 cups all-purpose flour
1/3 cup sugar
1 tablespoon baking powder
1/2 teaspoon salt
1/2 cup cold, unsalted butter, cut into small cubes
2/3 cup light cream

1. Preheat the oven to 425°. Line a baking sheet with parchment paper.

2. In a bowl, combine the flour, sugar, baking powder, and salt. Using a pastry blender or fork, cut in the butter until the texture of coarse meal. Add the cream and stir until the dough begins to come together.

3. Turn the dough out onto a lightly floured board and knead the dough into a ball. Form into a 3/4-inch thick round. Cut into 6ths. Place on the prepared baking sheet, 2 inches apart.

NOTATIONS

4. Bake for 13 to 15 minutes until lightly golden. Remove the scones to a rack to cool.

5. To serve, split the scones in half (like a bagel). Place the bottom halves on individual plates. Spread spoonfuls of the mascarpone cream onto the biscuits. Spoon the berries and their juice over the filling. Cover with the biscuit tops and present.

6 portions

PECAN STICKY BUNS

NOTATIONS

Who doesn't love a cinnamon sticky bun? This stream-lined version uses a shortbread pastry, rather than a yeast dough, making it easier to prepare. The buns are filled with cinnamon, brown sugar, and pecans, baked until gooey and delicious, and cloaked with a caramel glaze. These definitely have the WOW factor! Don't be put off by the length of the recipe—each section can be prepared in stages, making it easy to put together. It's definitely worth the effort.

Base:
2/3 cup packed dark brown sugar
2/3 cup heavy cream
1 teaspoon vanilla
1/2 cup chopped pecans

1. Preheat the oven to 350°. Grease a 9-inch square baking pan.

2. In a small mixing bowl, combine the sugar, cream, and vanilla, stirring until well mixed. Stir in the pecans. Pour the mixture into the prepared pan, spreading it evenly.

Filling:
1/4 cup packed dark brown sugar
2 tablespoons granulated sugar mixed with 2 teaspoons cinnamon
1/4 cup finely chopped pecans

In a small bowl, combine the brown sugar and granulated sugar and mix well. Stir in the pecans. (This may be made up to 3 days in advance and kept in an air-tight container.)

Dough:
2 3/4 cups all-purpose flour
1 teaspoon baking powder
1 teaspoon baking soda
1/2 teaspoon salt
2 tablespoons granulated sugar
6 tablespoons unsalted butter, melted and cooled
1 cup buttermilk
1 tablespoon unsalted butter, melted

NOTATIONS

1. In a large bowl, combine the flour, baking powder, baking soda, salt, and sugar and mix well. Add the 6 tablespoons melted butter and buttermilk and stir until the mixture comes together and forms a ball.

2. Turn the dough out onto a lightly floured board. Roll into a 9 x 12-inch rectangle. Brush the dough with 1 tablespoon melted butter.

3. Sprinkle the filling evenly over the melted butter. Starting on the long side, roll the dough up jelly-roll fashion, forming a log. Press gently to secure. Cut the log in half; then cut each half into 6 pieces. Place each piece in the pan, spiral side up, spacing evenly—3 rows of dough with 4 pieces in each row.

4. Bake for 20 to 25 minutes until lightly golden. Let cool for 1 minute; then invert the pan onto a large platter and let sit for 1 minute. Lift off the pan, scraping off any remaining glaze from the pan, and spreading it onto any bald areas of the rolls. Serve warm or at room temperature. These are best eaten the same day as made.

12 buns

CHOCOLATE INDULGENCES

NOTATIONS

CHOCOLATE CHIP WONTON CRISPS

Wonton skins are the perfect vehicle as a cookie base. Dusted with cinnamon and sugar and encrusted with chocolate chips, these light and crispy wafers are a sweet treat. Easy to prepare, these are your go-to chocolate chippers.

24 wonton wraps
2 tablespoons unsalted butter, melted
1/4 cup sugar mixed with 1 teaspoon cinnamon
1/2 cup plus 2 tablespoons mini semi-sweet chocolate chips

1. Preheat the oven to 400°.

2. Lay the wonton skins out on two baking pans, 1/2 inch apart.

3. Brush each generously with the melted butter. Dust with the cinnamon-sugar mixture. Sprinkle with the chocolate chips.

4. Bake for 6 to 7 minutes until golden. Remove the cookies from the pans to racks to cool.

24 crisps

CHOCOLATE-GLAZED MATZOH

NOTATIONS

This Passover holiday specialty item can be enjoyed by all. Matzoh provides the base for a caramelized chocolate-nut topping that keeps you coming back for more.

4 sheets matzoh
6 tablespoons unsalted butter, melted
1/2 cup dark brown sugar
1/2 cup finely chopped pecans
1/2 cup mini semi-sweet chocolate chips

1. Preheat the oven to 400°. Line two baking sheets with foil.

2. In a small bowl, combine the butter and sugar and stir until evenly mixed. Spread 2 tablespoons of the mixture on each piece of matzoh.

3. Sprinkle each piece with 2 tablespoons of chopped nuts. Place two pieces of matzoh on each baking sheet.

4. Bake for 5 to 6 minutes until golden and bubbly. Remove from the oven and immediately sprinkle each piece of matzoh with 2 tablespoons chocolate chips. Let sit for 1 minute; then spread the melted chocolate evenly over the matzoh. Place on racks to cool or refrigerate for 30 minutes to set the chocolate.

5. Break each sheet into 4 pieces.

4 portions

NOTATIONS

OUTRAGEOUS BROWNIE-NUT COOKIES

I guess the name says it all. These are like eating a brownie in cookie form. Fudgy, rich, moist, and chock full of walnuts, this chocolate experience brings home the blue ribbon.

4 tablespoons unsalted butter
14-ounce can sweetened condensed milk
16 ounces semi-sweet chocolate chips
1 teaspoon vanilla
1 cup all-purpose flour
pinch of salt
1½ cups coarsely chopped walnuts

1. Preheat the oven to 350°.

2. In a saucepan, gently heat the butter, condensed milk, and chocolate, stirring occasionally until the chocolate is melted and smooth. Remove from the heat and stir in the vanilla, flour, salt, and nuts. Mix well until evenly combined.

3. Using 1½ tablespoonfuls of dough, drop the batter onto ungreased baking sheets, 2 inches apart.

4. Bake for 8 to 10 minutes until set and no longer shiny on top. Let the cookies sit on the baking sheets for 2 minutes before removing them to racks to cool.

3½ dozen cookies

CHOCOLATE CHIP FOGGIES

NOTATIONS

Derived from the heavenly Seven Layer Bar recipe in my ***Home Cooking,*** these lacy, crispy, chewy cookies rival the infamous chocolate chip cookie in popularity.

$1\frac{1}{4}$ cups graham cracker crumbs
$\frac{1}{2}$ cup unsalted butter, melted
1 cup sweetened, shredded coconut
1 cup semi-sweet chocolate chips
1 cup white chocolate chips
2 cups chopped pecans
14-ounce can sweetened condensed milk

1. Preheat the oven to 350°. Line two baking sheets with parchment paper.

2. In a large mixing bowl, combine the graham cracker crumbs and butter, mixing until evenly moist. Stir in the coconut, chocolate chips, nuts, and condensed milk.

3. Using $1\frac{1}{2}$ tablespoonfuls of dough, drop the batter onto the baking sheets, 2 inches apart.

4. Bake for 8 to 10 minutes until the edges are golden. Let the cookies sit on the baking sheets for 3 minutes before removing them to racks to cool.

50 cookies

NOTATIONS

CHOCOLATE BROWNIE BISCOTTI

Classic brownie ingredients and flavors are encased in this biscotti presentation, making these pastries unique.

1/2 cup unsalted butter, at room temperature
1 cup sugar
2 eggs
1 teaspoon vanilla
1 tablespoon instant coffee powder
2 cups all-purpose flour
1/2 cup unsweetened cocoa
1/2 teaspoon baking powder
3/4 teaspoon baking soda
1/2 teaspoon salt
1 cup mini semi-sweet chocolate chips

1. Preheat the oven to 325°. Line two baking sheets with parchment paper.

2. In a large bowl with an electric mixer, cream the butter and sugar. Add the eggs, vanilla, and coffee and mix until evenly combined.

3. Add the flour, cocoa, baking powder, baking soda, and salt and mix well.

4. Stir in the chocolate chips.

5. Divide the dough in half. Turn each half out onto a baking sheet and form into a log, 3 inches wide and 12 inches long.

6. Bake for 30 minutes. Lift the parchment paper with the logs from the baking sheets to a board to cool for 5 minutes. Slice each log into 16 pieces (3/4-inch wide). Place a rack on each cookie sheet and place the slices on the racks, 1/2-inch apart.

7. Return the cookies to the oven and bake for 15 minutes more. Remove the racks from the baking sheets and let the biscotti cool completely. Store in an air-tight tin.

32 biscotti

WHITE CHOCOLATE CHIP-CHOCOLATE CRINKLES

NOTATIONS

These crinkles are the inverse of the ever popular chocolate chip cookie. The chocolate-rich dough is plump with white chocolate chips, creating a most satisfying chocolate experience.

2 ounces unsweetened chocolate, chopped
1 tablespoon instant espresso coffee powder
1/4 cup unsalted butter, at room temperature
3/8 cup packed dark brown sugar
1/2 cup granulated sugar
2 eggs
1/2 teaspoon vanilla
1 cup all-purpose flour
1 teaspoon baking powder
1/4 teaspoon salt
3/4 cup white chocolate chips
1/2 cup confectioners' sugar

1. In the top of a double boiler over simmering water, heat the chocolate and coffee powder, stirring until the chocolate is melted and smooth. Remove from the heat and let cool.

2. In a large bowl, cream the butter and sugars until fluffy. Add the eggs and vanilla and mix well. Add the cooled chocolate mixture, beating until completely incorporated.

3. Add the flour, baking powder, and salt and mix until evenly combined. Stir in the white chocolate chips.

4. Divide the dough in half and refrigerate for at least 4 hours and as much as overnight.

5. Preheat the oven to 350°. Line two baking sheets with parchment paper.

6. Remove half of the dough and roll into 1 1/4-inch balls. (The dough is somewhat sticky as it warms to room temperature, so it's best to keep the second half cold while working on the first half.) Roll in the confectioners' sugar, coating generously. Place on the prepared baking sheets, 2 inches apart. (Repeat with the second half of the dough.)

7. Bake for 10 minutes until the tops are shiny and the edges are slightly firm. Let the cookies sit on the baking sheets for 3 minutes before removing them to racks to cool.

27 to 29 cookies

NOTATIONS

PISTACHIO, CRANBERRY, AND WHITE CHOCOLATE CHIP BARK

Some consider this dessert; others indulge in this like candy. Whatever your preference, this semi-sweet chocolate-based bark is a decadent mixture of nuts, fruit, and chocolate chips that will satisfy your every yearning.

2/3 cup dried cranberries
1/2 cup bittersweet chocolate chips
1/2 cup white chocolate chips
2/3 cup shelled pistachio nuts
1/4 cup diced, candied crystallized ginger
12 ounces semi-sweet chocolate, chopped

1. Line a 9-inch square pan with foil, letting the foil overhang two opposite sides.

2. Put the cranberries, chocolate chips, nuts, and candied ginger in a bowl and mix well.

3. In the top of a double boiler over simmering water, gently heat the semi-sweet chocolate until almost melted. Remove from the heat and stir until smooth. Let cool for 10 minutes.

4. Pour the melted chocolate over the chip and nut mixture, stirring until evenly coated. Spread the mixture evenly in the prepared pan. Refrigerate for 1 to 2 hours until set.

5. Remove the bark from the refrigerator and let come to room temperature. Using the foil overhang, lift the bark out of the pan. With a sharp chopping knife, cut into squares and serve. (It crumbles somewhat when cut—not to worry—use the crumbs atop your favorite ice cream!) Store the bark in an air-tight tin. Note—this freezes well.

25 pieces

CHOCOLATE TRUFFLE BARS

NOTATIONS

These bars are rich, velvety, and decadent. A graham cracker crust is host to an intense bittersweet chocolate truffle topping that's laced with liqueur. Personalize your bars by adding your favorite liqueur to the batter, making them extra-special.

Crust:
1¼ cups graham cracker crumbs
3 tablespoons sugar
5 tablespoons unsalted butter, melted

1. Preheat the oven to 350°. Line a 9-inch square pan with parchment paper, letting it overhang the pan on two opposite sides.

2. In a mixing bowl, combine the graham cracker crumbs, sugar, and butter and stir until evenly blended. Press the mixture firmly into the prepared pan.

3. Bake the crust for 10 minutes until lightly golden. Let cool completely.

Truffle Topping:
12 ounces bittersweet chocolate chips
½ cup heavy cream
2 tablespoons unsalted butter
1 tablespoon favorite liqueur (Amaretto, Crème de Cacao, Chambord, Grand Marnier, Kahlúa, rum to name a few)

1. In the top of a double boiler over simmering water, heat the chocolate, cream, and butter, stirring until the chocolate is melted and smooth. Remove from the heat and mix in the liqueur.

2. Pour the chocolate mixture onto the cooled, baked crust, spreading it evenly in the pan. Refrigerate for 2 hours until set. Using the parchment overhang, lift the mixture from the pan. Cut into bars and store in the refrigerator. Remove from the refrigerator 30 minutes before serving.

25 bars

ROCKY ROAD CLUSTERS

NOTATIONS

These peanut butter-infused chocolate squares are studded with mini marshmallows and Rice Krispies for pure pleasure. They appeal to the kid in all of us!

3 cups (18 ounces) semi-sweet chocolate chips
$1\frac{1}{2}$ cups chunky peanut butter
1 teaspoon vanilla
2 cups Rice Krispies cereal
3 cups mini marshmallows

1. Line a 9 x 13-inch pan with foil, letting it overhang the pan on each end. Grease the foil.

2. In the top of a double boiler over simmering water, melt the chocolate, stirring until smooth. Remove from the heat.

3. Add the peanut butter and vanilla and mix until evenly incorporated. Add the cereal and marshmallows and stir until evenly combined.

4. Spread the mixture in the prepared pan and refrigerate for 1 to 2 hours until set.

5. Using the foil overhang, lift the chocolate out of the pan. Cut into bars and serve. Store any extra in an air-tight container.

48 bars

FROSTED CHOCOLATE-WALNUT BROWNIES

NOTATIONS

I'm turning up the volume on these already decadent nut-encrusted brownies by frosting them with a chocolate ganache. It's chocolate nirvana and it doesn't get better than this!

4 ounces unsweetened chocolate, chopped
1 cup unsalted butter
1 tablespoon instant coffee powder
2 cups sugar
3 eggs
1 teaspoon vanilla
1 cup all-purpose flour
¼ teaspoon salt
1 cup chopped walnuts
Chocolate Ganache (recipe follows)

1. Preheat the oven to 350°. Line the bottom of a 9-inch square pan with parchment paper letting it overhang the pan on two opposite sides. Grease the exposed sides of the pan.

2. In the top of a double boiler over simmering water, heat the chocolate, butter, and coffee powder, stirring until the chocolate is melted and smooth. Remove from the heat and let cool.

3. In a bowl with an electric mixer, beat the sugar and eggs until pale lemon colored. Add the vanilla and the cooled chocolate and beat until evenly mixed.

4. Add the flour and salt and mix well. Stir in the walnuts. Pour into the prepared pan.

5. Bake for 40 minutes until the top is crusty and a toothpick inserted in the center comes out slightly moist. Place on a rack to cool completely.

6. Pour the chocolate ganache over the cooled brownies, spreading it evenly over the top. Refrigerate for 1 to 2 hours until firm. Using the parchment overhang, lift the brownies from the pan. Cut into squares and serve. (Any uneaten brownies should be stored in the refrigerator.)

25 squares

NOTATIONS

Chocolate Ganache:
5 tablespoons heavy cream
4 ounces semi-sweet chocolate, chopped
2 tablespoons crème fraîche

In a small saucepan, warm the cream until hot—do not let it come to a boil. Remove from the heat and add the chocolate, stirring until the chocolate is melted and smooth. Stir in the crème fraîche.

CHOCOLATE MOUSSE

NOTATIONS

This light mousse boasts a trio of chocolates—unsweetened, milk, and cocoa powder—making it perfectly chocolaty. Adding vanilla to the batter is a good counterpoint to the chocolate, as it enhances its depth of flavor. I like to garnish the mousse with a dollop of sweetened whipped cream.

¾ cup whole milk
8 ounces milk chocolate, chopped
3 ounces unsweetened baking chocolate, chopped
3 tablespoons unsweetened cocoa
4 cups miniature marshmallows
1 teaspoon vanilla
1 cup heavy cream

1. In a 2-quart saucepan, heat the milk, chocolates, cocoa, and marshmallows over low until melted, stirring often. Remove from the heat.

2. Stir in the vanilla and let cool to room temperature.

3. In the bowl of an electric mixer, whip the cream to soft peaks. Gently fold the whipped cream into the cooled chocolate mixture.

4. Spoon the mousse into individual ramekins and refrigerate until serving time. (This may be made up to 24 hours in advance.)

5. When ready to serve, garnish each with a dollop of sweetened whipped cream and raspberries.

6 portions

NOTATIONS

CHOCOLATE GANACHE CRÈME

This chocolate extravaganza is the closest thing to heaven. Reminiscent of a truffle, it's outrageously chocolaty, rich, and intense. This is truly the ultimate chocolate dessert.

1½ cups heavy cream
1 tablespoon instant coffee powder
12 ounces best quality bittersweet chocolate, chopped
1 teaspoon vanilla

1. In the top of a double boiler over simmering water, heat the cream and coffee powder—do not let it boil. Add the chocolate and stir constantly until the chocolate melts and is very smooth. Remove from the heat. Stir in the vanilla.

2. Pour the ganache into 8 small ramekins. Cover and refrigerate until set and chilled, at least 1 hour and as much as 2 days.

3. Remove the ganache from the refrigerator 30 minutes before serving. Garnish each portion with a small scoop of vanilla ice cream and enjoy!

8 portions

REVISITING CHOCOLATE PUDDING CAKE

NOTATIONS

What do you say about a chocolate pudding cake that describes it properly? That it's rich, fudgy, and decadent? It's all that and more. During the baking stage, the cake forms its own fudge sauce that puts this dessert over the top. The addition of vanilla and coffee flavors actually enhances the deep chocolate taste. This updated version from my ***Home Cooking*** is even better this time around.

Cake:
1 cup all-purpose flour
3/4 cup sugar
1/4 cup unsweetened cocoa
1 tablespoon instant coffee powder
2 teaspoons baking powder
1/2 teaspoon salt
1/2 cup whole milk
4 tablespoons unsalted butter, melted
1 teaspoon vanilla

Pudding:
3/4 cup light brown sugar
1/4 cup unsweetened cocoa
1 1/4 cups boiling water

1. Preheat the oven to 350°.

2. In a large mixing bowl, combine the flour, sugar, cocoa, coffee, baking powder, and salt and mix well.

3. Add the milk, butter, and vanilla and stir until evenly mixed. Transfer the mixture to an ungreased 8-inch square pan, spreading it evenly in the pan.

4. Make the pudding. In a small bowl, combine the brown sugar and cocoa and stir until evenly mixed. Add the boiling water and stir until the cocoa is dissolved. Pour this mixture over the cake batter—do not stir!

5. Bake for about 35 minutes until the top is set. Let cool for 15 minutes—the pudding thickens as it cools. Serve warm with the pudding spooned over the cake.

8 portions

BEYOND FUDGE CAKE

NOTATIONS

Chocoholics take heed. This is probably the richest, most fudgy, decadent chocolate cake this side of heaven! It will leave your taste buds begging for more.

12 ounces bittersweet chocolate
2 tablespoons instant coffee powder
5 eggs, separated
1¼ cups sugar
1 cup unsalted butter, at room temperature
1 teaspoon vanilla
¾ cup all-purpose flour
pinch of salt

1. Preheat the oven to 350°. Line the bottom of a 9-inch springform pan with parchment paper. Grease the parchment paper and the sides of the pan.

2. In the top of a double boiler over simmering water, heat the chocolate and coffee powder, stirring until the chocolate is melted and smooth. Remove from the heat and let cool.

3. In a medium-size bowl, beat the egg whites until frothy. Gradually add ¼ cup sugar, beating until stiff peaks form. Set aside.

4. In a large mixing bowl, cream the butter and 1 cup sugar. Add the egg yolks and vanilla and beat until thick and pale lemon colored.

5. Add the cooled chocolate, mixing until evenly blended. Mix in the flour and salt.

6. By hand, gently fold in 1/3 of the stiffly beaten egg whites into the chocolate mixture to lighten the batter. Add the remaining beaten whites, folding gently until no traces of white remain. Turn the batter into the prepared pan, smoothing the top surface with a spatula.

7. Bake for 40 minutes or until a toothpick inserted in the center comes out slightly moist and the top of the cake is slightly cracked. Remove to a rack to cool completely.

8. Run a knife around the edge of the pan. Unmold the cake and serve. I like to garnish the cake with sweetened whipped cream.

10 portions

MARY'S CHOCOLATE MAYONNAISE CAKE

NOTATIONS

This rendition steps up the old-fashioned 50s version to gourmet heights. Mayonnaise in a cake you ask? Mayonnaise is basically eggs and oil, thus replacing the need for those ingredients in the batter. The mayonnaise actually helps to make the cake moist and fluffy. This ultra chocolaty cake with its Kahlúa butter cream frosting gets a 5-star rating in our family.

1½ cups sugar
⅔ cup Dutch processed cocoa
1 tablespoon instant coffee powder
2 teaspoons vanilla
1 cup real mayonnaise (Don't use low-fat or non-fat versions.)
2 cups all-purpose flour
1 teaspoon baking soda
¼ teaspoon salt
1⅓ cups water
⅔ cup bittersweet chocolate chips
Kahlúa Butter Cream (recipe follows)
1 to 2 tablespoons shaved semi-sweet chocolate for garnish

1. Preheat the oven to 350°. Grease a 9-inch square baking pan.

2. In a bowl with an electric mixer, blend together the sugar, cocoa, and coffee powder. Add the vanilla and mayonnaise and mix until evenly combined.

3. Sift together the flour, baking soda, and salt. Add the dry ingredients alternately with the water to the batter. Stir in the chocolate chips.

4. Turn the batter into the prepared pan.

5. Bake for 40 minutes until a toothpick inserted in the center comes out slightly moist and fudgy. Place on a rack to cool completely. Frost with the Kahlúa butter cream and decorate with shaved chocolate before serving. (Store any uneaten cake in the refrigerator.)

9 to 12 portions

NOTATIONS

Kahlúa Butter Cream:

2 cups confectioners' sugar
4 tablespoons unsalted butter, at room temperature
1 tablespoon heavy cream
2 to 3 tablespoons Kahlúa

In a bowl with an electric mixer, cream the sugar and butter until fluffy. Add the cream and Kahlúa and beat until smooth. Refrigerate until needed.

CHOCOLATE-NUT TORTE

NOTATIONS

Outrageous and seductive only begin to describe this flourless chocolate torte. A shortbread base houses a rich, fudgy, walnut-encrusted chocolate filling that's sublime. This absolutely tops the charts for chocolate experiences!

Crust:
1 cup all-purpose flour
1/2 cup cold unsalted butter, cut into small cubes
1/4 cup sugar

1. Preheat the oven to 350°. Grease a 9-inch springform pan.

2. Put the flour, butter, and sugar in the bowl of a food processor and pulse until the texture of coarse meal. Remove the mixture to the springform and press it firmly onto the bottom and half way up the sides of the pan.

Filling:
12 ounces semi-sweet chocolate, chopped
1/2 cup heavy cream
3/4 cup dark brown sugar
1/4 cup dark corn syrup
1 1/2 teaspoons vanilla
pinch of salt
3 eggs, beaten
2 1/2 cups coarsely chopped walnuts

1. In the top of a double boiler over simmering water, heat the chocolate and cream, stirring until the chocolate is melted and smooth. Remove from the heat, add the brown sugar, corn syrup, vanilla, and salt, and mix well.

2. Let cool; then stir in the eggs. Add the nuts and mix until evenly combined.

3. Pour the mixture onto the prepared crust, smoothing the batter evenly.

4. Bake for 45 minutes. Remove to a rack to cool until set, then refrigerate for 2 or more hours until firm. Remove the form from the bottom of the pan, slice the torte, and serve.

12 or more portions

MENU SUGGESTIONS

MEDITERRANEAN REPAST
Cucumber Cups Mediterranée
Grilled Chicken with Muhammara
Chickpea and Parsley Salad
Mixed Greens with Olive Vinaigrette
Pistachio Biscotti

WINE AND . . .
Lemon-Thyme Biscotti
Wontons Balazar
Crab Tartlets
Dates Rogère
Stuffed Mushrooms Italiano

SPANISH SAMPLER
Sangría
Apple, Manchego, and Membrillo Napoleons
Mango Gazpacho
Grilled Steak with Romesco Sauce
Tapas Salad

MOVIE MARATHON
Tomato Bruschetta
Roasted Green Olives
Polenta Fries
Lacquered Salami
Sausages and Clams

THANKSGIVING DINNER
Sausage-Stuffed Mushrooms
Pumpkin Soup
Roast Turkey with Favorite Stuffing
The Cape Codder
Deep-Dish Cranberry-Nut Pie
Ginger Cream Cake

SOUTH-OF-THE-BORDER LUNCH
Avocado Dip
Shrimp with Chipotle Mayonnaise
Mexican-Style Caesar
Lime Shortbread

PICNIC IN THE PARK
White Bean Dip
Pasta with Eggplant Relish
Prosciutto-Wrapped Chicken
Outrageous Brownie-Nut Cookies

ASIAN TIDBITS
Mushrooms Teriyaki
Crab Rangoon Revisited
Shrimp Toasts
Pork Balls in Lettuce Pockets

MOTHER'S DAY BRUNCH

Raspberry Bellini
Apricots St. Germain
Baby Greens with Pomegranate-Molasses Vinaigrette
Blue Cheese-Spinach Strata
Mixed Berry Shortcakes

BACKYARD BARBECUE

Chili Dip
Grilled Burgers with Stuffed Roma Tomatoes
Coleslaw Henri
Warm German-Style Potato Salad
Congo Bars

DINNER AL FRESCO

Deviled Bluefish Pâté
Crab Salad
Reds and Greens
Chocolate Ganache Crème

WEDDING SHOWER LUNCHEON

Cucumber Bruschetta
Lemon Fricos
Egg Salad and Endive
Salad Marché
Lobster, Corn, and Tomato Salad
Strawberries and Cream Baby Cakes

TAILGATING

Green Olive Hummus
Jazzy Hard-Boiled Eggs
Glazed Chicken Wings
Couscous Salad
Cranberry-Pecan Grahams

TEA TIME

Apple-Cheddar Puffs
Toasted Peanut Butter and Jelly Sandwiches
Date Nuggets
Pecan Shortbread

MEZE PARTY

Marcona Almonds
Roasted Kalamatas
Pumpkin Hummus
Falafel
Spanokopita Tartlets
Herbed Feta Crostini

SUNDAY BRUNCH

Pomosas
Spinach and Goat Cheese Frittata
Smoked Salmon Tartare
Pecan Sticky Buns
Lemon Cream Cake

BOOK CLUB

Figs Celeste
Pasta with Roasted Sausages and Grapes
Caesar Salad Revisited
Yellow Cake with Chocolate Frosting

SUPER BOWL BASH

Dark and Stormies
Palomas
Poppers
Meatballs Marinara
Grilled Sausages with Mango Mustard

HORS D'OEUVRES FOR TWELVE

Cranberry-Chèvre Spread
Bruschetta with Ricotta and Fig Jam
Salami Crisps
Shrimp with Mango Salsa
Couscous Cakes
Lamb Lollypops

LADIES WHO LUNCH

Strawberry Soup
Chopped Cobb Salad
Herbed Mini Scones
Lemon Coeur à la Crème

INDEX

W

Y

Z

Made in the USA
Las Vegas, NV
11 December 2021

37192273R00055